IMAGINARIUM

Imag·i·nar·i·um

(*noun*) a place devoted to the imagination.

JOHN HUNT PUBLISHING

First published by Our Street Books, 2023
Our Street Books is an imprint of John Hunt Publishing Ltd., No. 3 East Street, Alresford
Hampshire SO24 9EE, UK
office@jhpbooks.com
www.johnhuntpublishing.com
www.ourstreet-books.com

For distributor details and how to order please visit the 'Ordering' section on our website.

ISBN: 978 1 84694 089 7
978 1 84694 421 5 (ebook)
Library of Congress Control Number: 2021946233

A CIP catalogue record for this book is available from the British Library.

Advisory Editor: Anthea Church

Design: Amber Sutton (Relax Kids)
Design Assistant: Frankie Taylor

Gutenberg Press

UK: Printed and bound by CPI Group (UK) Ltd, Croydon, CR0 4YY
Printed in North America by CPI GPS partners

To the amazing teenage football team in Thailand, who were trapped in the cave for eighteen days with just water to drink (June 2018).

I was following your story as I wrote this book and was so inspired by your fighting spirit and ability to stay calm in such a difficult situation. I hope you continue to use the meditation skills you learnt in the cave and teach us all how you did it.
You are unbelievably amazing!

Contents

Chamber of Beliefs
Chamber of Safety
Chamber of Happiness
Chamber of Kindness
Chamber of Solutions
Chamber of Acceptance
Chamber of Awareness
Chamber of Stress Management
Chamber of Choices
Chamber of Power
Chamber of Confidence
Chamber of Love
Chamber of Positivity
Chamber of Calm
Chamber of Support
Chamber of Dreams
Chamber of Discovery
Chamber of Boundaries
Chamber of Change
Chamber of Creativity
Chamber of emotions
Chamber of Sleep
Chamber of Appreciation
Chamber of Relaxation
Chamber of gratitude

Note from Marneta

For a few years now, I have wanted to write a book that explores the different chambers of the mind. I love the idea that our mind is an amazing resource, just waiting for us to use. We have everything we need at our finger tips. We can enquire, explore, visualise and even time travel.

Before I wrote the book, I asked parents on the Relax Kids Facebook groups what they felt were the biggest issues teens faced and what support they needed most. There were over one hundred comments and I felt a little daunted by the task ahead.

The meditations in this book have been created to introduce young people to meditation and relaxation techniques as they explore the corners of their own minds. It aims to help them enjoy spending time alone and start to build an inner world. This book allows young people to take back their power by using the power of their mind and thoughts.

I hope this book brings much needed support and reassurance to young people. I also hope the exercises help support every single issue that was on that Facebook list.

Heartfelt thanks to my dearest friends Rowena, Ana, Anthea, Gill and Jamie and all the young people who tested the chambers in Oxford. Your wise thoughts and suggestions were so valuable. I am so grateful for your friendship.

This book can be used as a resource for the Relax Kids ChargeUp programme that helps young people develop vital tools to help them navigate life's issues.

Foreword/Preface

During the last thirty years of my teaching career, I have noticed a marked difference in the emotional well-being of my students, even those from the most privileged backgrounds. For reasons described frequently in the media, young people seem less able to concentrate, they worry more, are more often absent, sleepless or agitated. Of course, they continue to delight with their unfailing sense of humour but there is a quickness to cynicism which results perhaps from the fact that they are often called to observe, even be a part of, too much too soon.

At Kent College in Pembury, we have responded to this by introducing regular timetabled lessons in sport and well-being. Not being a sportswoman myself, I have chosen to work with sixth formers on emotional health. For this, I have used exercises that I have devised for myself, as well as Marneta's 'Imaginarium'. What has struck us all in the process is how rich a resource the mind is. While the world might look bleak, most minds, if guided, have lost none of their capacity to imagine, visualise and heal.

This is a wonderful book for young people, a workbook for teachers, and a resource for anyone of any age who is trying to strengthen themselves emotionally. Its great virtue lies in the fact that it does not pedal a cultish philosophy but offers the mind activities which will help it to draw its own conclusions as to how to redress imbalances, face obstacles, and renew itself. This is an invaluable resource for which as a teacher, I am enormously grateful.

Anthea Church
December 2018

Disclaimer:

Beginners meditation and relaxation is generally considered a safe activity. In ChargeUp, we only use simple relaxation techniques. However, if young people have a history of mental illness, then please consult with your health care provider.

Please be aware that Relax Kids Ltd, Relax Kids coaches and ChargeUp coaches make no claim to be any kind of medical professionals, psychologists, therapists, or counsellors.

Relax Kids can accept no responsibility for any adverse affects, direct or indirect, that may result from your use of the information in this book. By using this book, you agree that you use the information contained in these exercises entirely at your own discretion.

If trauma has been experienced, please see a trained therapist for extended support.

Supporting Children's Wellbeing
relax Kids
SINCE 2000

DISSOCIATED
Chamber of Awareness p21

CONFLICTED
Chamber of Emotions p51
Chamber of Choices p111

AMBIVALENT
Chamber of Support p99

MISUNDERSTOOD
Chamber of Acceptance p147
Chamber of Discovery p15

WORTHLESS
Chamber of Beliefs p141
Chamber of Kindness p153
Chamber of Love p63

REJECTE
Chamber of Love

ANXIOUS
Chamber of Calm p27

FEARFUL
Chamber of Power p75
Chamber of Safety p135

UNRESTED
Chamber of Sleep p45
Chamber of Relaxation p39

TENSE
Chamber of Relaxation p39

ANGRY
Chamber of Calm p27
Chamber of Acceptance p147
Chamber of Stress-Management
Chamber of Boundaries p117

EMOTIONAL
Chamber of Emotions p51

LONELY
Chamber of Love p63
Chamber of Support p99

LOST
Chamber of Emotions p51
Chamber of Acceptance p147
Chamber of Awareness p21
Chamber of Discovery p15
Chamber of Choices p111

UNCONFIDENT
Chamber of Confidence p57

NEGATIVE
Chamber of Happiness p93
Chamber of Positivity p87
Chamber of Kindness p153

TORN
Chamber of Choices p111
Chamber of Emotions p51
Chamber of Solutions p123

HOPELESS
Chamber of Dreams p161
Chamber of Power p75
Chamber of Solutions p123

HUMILITATED
Chamber of Power p75
Chamber of Solutions p123

ASHAMED
Chamber of Acceptance p147
Chamber of Beliefs p141
Chamber of Kindness p153

ALIENATED
Chamber of Kindness p153
Chamber of Love p63

LOW SELF-ESTEEM
Chamber of Confidence p57
Chamber of Acceptance p147
Chamber of Gratitude p105
Chamber of Power p75
Chamber of Appreciation p69

ANNOYED
Chamber of Boundaries p117
Chamber of Stress-Management p33
Chamber of Calm p27

FRUSTRATED
Chamber of Stress-Management p33
Chamber of Choices p111
Chamber of Relaxation p39

INSECURE
Chamber of Safety p135
Chamber of Love p63
Chamber of Kindness p153
Chamber of Appreciation p69

SELF CONSCIOUS
Chamber of Beliefs p141
Chamber of Confidence p57

UNSUPPORTED
Chamber of Support p99

How do you feel today?

Use this map to help you find which chamber to visit.

UNSAFE
- Chamber of Safety p135

ABANDONED
- Chamber of Support p99
- Chamber of Love p63

AGITATED
- Chamber of Awareness p21
- Chamber of Emotions p51
- Chamber of Support p99
- Chamber of Relaxation p39

JEALOUS
- Chamber of Appreciation p69
- Chamber of Gratitude p105

SAD
- Chamber of Happiness p93
- Chamber of Positivity p87

NERVOUS
- Chamber of Confidence p57
- Chamber of Support p99
- Chamber of Power p75

UNCREATIVE
- Chamber of Creativity p129
- Chamber of Discovery p15
- Chamber of Dreams p161

UNCOMFORTABLE
- Chamber of Boundaries p117
- Chamber of Relaxation p39

ALONE
- Chamber of Love p63
- Chamber of Support p99
- Chamber of Safety p135
- Chamber of Kindness p153

SELF-CRITICAL
- Chamber of Beliefs p141
- Chamber of Acceptance p147

WORRIED
- Chamber of Safety p135
- Chamber of Solutions p123
- Chamer of Calm p27

MISERABLE
- Chamber of Love p63
- Chamber of Happiness p93
- Chamber of Gratitude p105

GRIEF
- Chamber of Support p99
- Chamber of Love p63
- Chamber of Change p81

EMBARRASSED
- Chamber of Beliefs p141
- Chamber of Kindness p153

HEARTBROKEN
- Chamber of Choices p111
- Chamber of Love p63
- Chamber of Support p99
- Chamber of Change p81

FATIGUED
- Chamber of Sleep p45

DISAPPOINTED
- Chamber of Acceptance p147
- Chamber of Gratitude p105

RESENTFUL
- Chamber of Gratitude p105

ISOLATED
- Chamber of Support p99

SELF-HATRED
- Chamber of Acceptance p147
- Chamber of Gratitude p105
- Chamber of Appreciation p69
- Chamber of Love p63

BORED
- Chamber of Discovery p15
- Chamber of Creativity p129
- Chamber of Appreciation p69

OVERWHELMED
- Chamber of Stress-Management p33
- Chamber of Emotions p51
- Chamber of Boundaries p117

INADEQUATE
- Chamber of Love p63
- Chamber of Confidence p57
- Chamber of Kindness p153

SHY
- Chamber of Confidence p57

CHAMBER OF DISCOVERY

"Knowing yourself is the beginning of all wisdom." - *Aristotle*

CHAMBER OF DISCOVERY

Close your eyes, breathe in slowly, release your shoulders and relax. Turn your thoughts inwards and focus inside your head.

How does your head feel? Crammed with information? Tight and tense with tension? Tired? Take in a deep breath and as you breathe out, let the tension go. Make some space inside your head. Feel a sense of expansion. Feel the tightness and tension slipping away. Breathe in expansion, breathe out tension. Breathe in, breathe out.

Inside your head is one of the most complex and sophisticated structures in the universe. An incredible machine with over a hundred billion nerve cells and a hundred trillion nerve connections, your brain is the control centre for all your bodily functions, such as walking, talking and breathing. The mind is the invisible part of your brain that is in control of your thinking, feeling, beliefs, perceptions and understanding. Your brain is even more complex and incredible than your mobile phone. It stores every memory, piece of data and records each one of your experiences. You are now going to take a tour of the mysterious interior of your mind.

Imagine it as a building full of winding corridors. While lying in bed or on waking, even when just sitting, experiment with walking down the corridors, noticing a wide variety of doors that lead to a multitude of chambers. Breathe in deeply and allow your body and mind to become relaxed and curious. The more relaxed and curious you are, the more easily you will be able to explore.

As you wander along the corridors, notice the doors leading to all the chambers. It is in these chambers that you will make some of the most important discoveries about your being. For the sake of this exercise we are going to give these chambers names, for example the Chamber of Gratitude, Chamber of Happiness, Chamber of Creativity and the Chamber of Beliefs.

All these chambers represent the qualities you have inside. Each door is closed and ready for further exploration. Notice you are holding a bunch of keys. Each key is labelled with the name of a chamber. You feel full of curiosity and interest as you pass the different chambers, wondering what is behind the locked doors.

As you move along the corridors, feel every corner of every corridor filling with light. It is a cooling light that helps you feel calm and in control. Breathe in and and slowly breathe out. Breathe in, breathe out. Notice how your mind begins to fill with this cooling light. Breathe in, breathe out, breathe in, breathe out, breathe in, breathe out. Feel the light moving through your head. Notice how the light seems to be creating more space. Feel the space, feel the expansion and feel the clarity.

"I am curious; I am curious."

Write or draw how you feel in your **CHAMBER OF DISCOVERY**

QUESTIONS TO ASK YOURSELF:

What new feelings did I discover?

What new things about myself did I discover today?

What am I curious about?

ACTION:

Keep a note book and write down any new thoughts and discoveries you find out about yourself as you continue to work through this book.

MY DISCOVERIES

Write down all the new discoveries you have made about yourself, others and life.

CHAMBER OF AWARENESS

"Your mind will answer most questions if you learn to relax and wait for the answer." *– William S. Burroughs*

CHAMBER OF AWARENESS

Close your eyes, breathe in slowly, release your shoulders and relax. Walk through the corridors of your mind until you come to the Chamber of Awareness. Find the correct key, turn the lock, open the door and step inside.

On the floor, in the middle of the chamber is an X. Stand on it and notice the body scanner is activating. As it activates, a screen lights up in front of you which in turn shows your body lighting up. Follow the instructions on the screen that ask you to take in a deep breath for the count of four and breathe out to the count of six. Breathe in, breathe out.

The screen in front of you lights up different parts of your body, showing you where you need to be more aware. You see a light on the nose area. Notice how your breath feels as it comes in through your nose. Notice how cool or warm it is. The chest area is lighting up on the screen. Become aware of your lungs filling up with air and then gently letting go.

You see the stomach area lighting up in front of you. Notice how your stomach feels. Do you feel any sensation in your stomach? Can you feel any tension or tightness?

Now, the shoulder areas light up on the screen. Notice how they feel as you become aware of your shoulders only. Do you feel any tightness there? Notice the tightness without any judgement. Notice how your clothes feel on your shoulder.

Next, your head is lighting up on the screen. Bring your awareness to your head and notice how it feels. Are there any areas of tension in your head? How does your head feel? Scan through your forehead, your eyes, ears, nose and mouth. Notice even the smallest of feelings which normally you might miss.

Now the screen is lighting up your hands. Notice how your hands feel. Do they feel warm or cold? Do they feel tense or relaxed? Notice how each finger feels.

Next come your feet. They are also showing up on the scanner. Notice how

your feet touch the floor. Which parts of your feet are touching the floor? Do they feel light of heavy? How do they feel in your shoes?
Spend a few more moments watching the screen in front of you light up various parts of the body at random. Continue to focus on your breathing and notice how each part of your body feels. Breathe in, breathe out; breathe in and breathe out.

Now, bring your awareness to your mind. Notice your thoughts. What are you thinking about? Where do your thoughts drift to? Watch your thoughts drifting past your mind. Breathe in and out and notice the thoughts moving across the screen of your mind. You are the observer watching your thoughts. As thoughts move past, let them go. Smile and let them pass as you stay aware and unaffected by them. If thoughts arise that bring you discomfort or make you feel uneasy, you can brush them away or gently dissolve the thought because you are the controller. Your awareness has put you back in the seat of power. You are in charge of your thoughts and so you can create new thoughts.

Stay for as long as you wish in this Chamber of Awareness.

When you are ready to leave, step off the X and move towards the door. On your way out, there is a portable scanner. You may take the scanner with you if you would like to scan for awareness at any point during the day. As you leave, remember that you can return to the Chamber of Awareness whenever you wish.

"I am aware; I am aware."

Write or draw how you feel in your **CHAMBER OF AWARENESS**

QUESTION TO ASK YOURSELF:

Think about an event that happened today and try and recall what was happening in your body (your temperature, your heart, your breathing, your limbs and your head) during the event? Think about how you felt before the event and how you felt after it.

ACTION:

Choose a part of your body such as your arms or your stomach and, while you are going about your daily activities, lightly focus on that part, registering what it is feeling. For example, does your stomach feel tight or tingly? Watch how the feeling changes.

Write in words or mark in colors to note down bodily sensations to help increase your awareness.

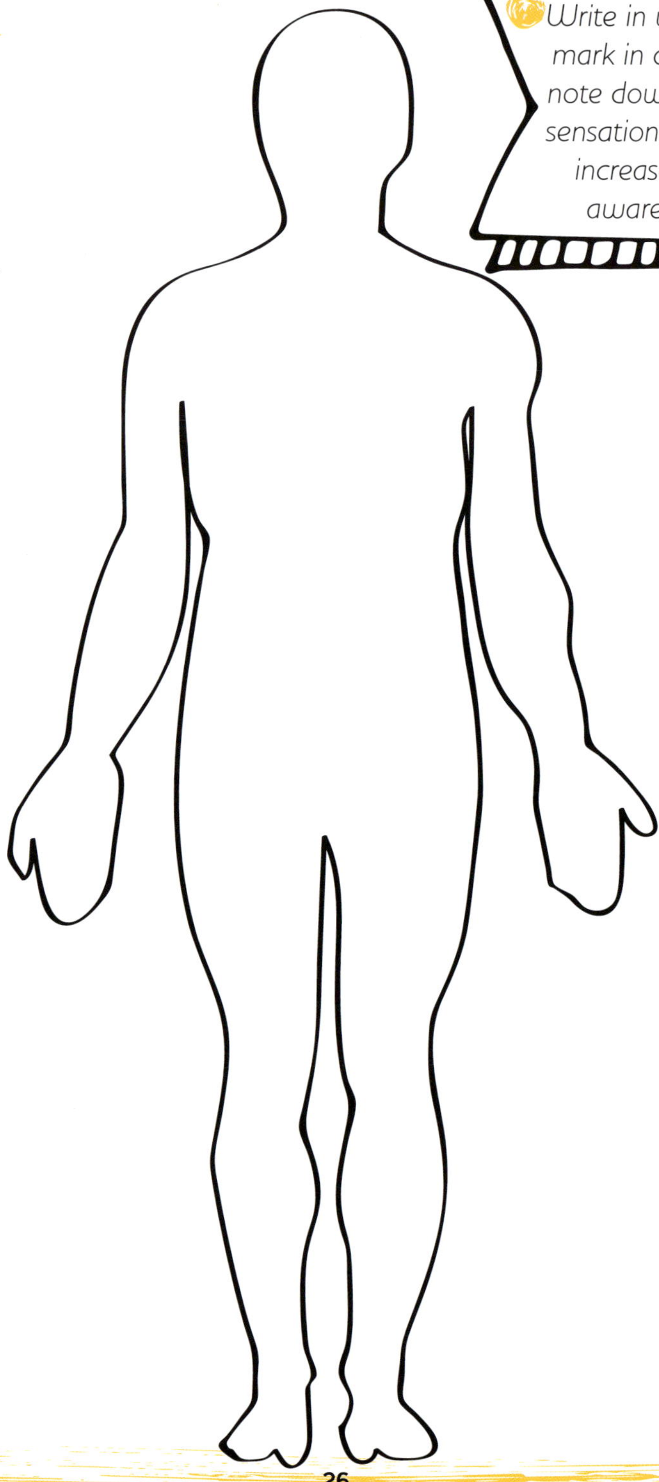

CHAMBER OF CALM

"Calm mind brings inner strength and self-confidence, so that's very important for good health."

- Dalai Lama

CHAMBER OF CALM

Close your eyes, breathe in slowly, release your shoulders and relax. Walk through the corridors of your mind until you come to the Chamber of Calm. Find the correct key, turn the lock, open the door and step inside.

The Chamber of Calm is a place that you can come to whenever you feel the need to stop, take a break, let go, relax and feel at peace. This is a place that is always here for you to visit in order to settle your nerves and chill out for a while. Step into the Chamber of Calm, remembering to put the DO NOT DISTURB sign on the door.

As soon as you enter into the chamber, you feel your whole body letting go and relaxing. You notice there is a pile of beanbags in the room. Sit or lie on the beanbags in any position you want. You can use as many of the beanbags as you like. There is also a huge fluffy blanket. Place it over you and set the dial to whatever temperature you wish. If you feel you need to cool off to relax and would prefer a cooler temperature, you can set it to cold, cool or mild. If you would prefer to feel warm and snuggly, you can set the temperature to warm, toasty or hot. Which temperature would you like the blanket to be?

Feel your body softening and relaxing into the beanbags. Notice where your body is touching the beanbags. Can you feel yourself sinking more and more deeply into the bags?

Lie under the blanket and feel its softness against your clothes and skin. Under the cool or warm blanket, notice the points of contact with your skin and the blanket. Notice where the blanket touches your arms and see if you can let your arms soften and relax. Notice where the blanket touches your legs and see if you can let your legs soften and relax. Is the blanket touching your stomach or back? Allow your back and stomach to completely relax. Let everything go. Notice how your body and mind are feeling more and more calm.

While you are lying there, you notice a remote control. This is a personal transportation device that can take you wherever you would like to go. On the remote, you notice a number of buttons with pictures or names of a variety of calming places. There is a forest, park, temple or place of worship, cave, garden, museum, desert, beach and mountain. There are also a couple of blank buttons where you can choose a special calming place of your own. Which calming place would you like to visit? Which place would help you feel the most calm and relaxed? Do you want to be outside in nature or would you prefer to be inside a quiet building such as a shed, cosy room or temple? The choice is yours and you can choose a different place each time. Take in three deep breaths and let them out slowly.

Press the remote control button and allow yourself to be transported in space and time to the new calming place. When you have arrived, take some time to look around and investigate the surroundings. As you move about, notice how you feel. Do you feel calm and safe? Do you feel relaxed and secure? Do you feel quiet and calm? If it is not what you expected, you always have the choice to press another button on the remote and transport yourself to a new place or even just take yourself back to the beautiful Chamber of Calm. Take in three deep breaths and let them out slowly.

Once you have investigated the new surroundings, you notice a table with paper, pencils, paints and coloring materials. Start to draw the place you are in, including as much detail as you can. Draw every part of your new surroundings. See if you can infuse the page with so much peace and calm that people looking at the picture will also feel a deep sense of calm. Take in three deep breaths and let them out slowly.

When you have finished, fold the paper and put it in your pocket. Prepare to return to the chamber and press the home button on the remote. You find yourself back in the chamber, lying on the beanbags snuggled under the cool or warm blanket.

When you are ready, stand up and walk out of the chamber, holding on to your picture of calm, knowing that you can return here whenever you feel you need to experience calm or want to chill, take some time out or relax for a while.

"I am calm; I am calm."

Write or draw how you feel in your **CHAMBER OF CALM**

QUESTIONS TO ASK YOURSELF:

What did I discover that helped me feel calm today?

Do I feel calm inside my body?

What activities can I do to make me feel calm?

ACTION:

Find a space that makes you feel calm (your bed or garden) and visit it whenever you need to.

CHOOSE SOMETHING TO HELP YOU FEEL CALM

MENU

- TENSE YOUR BODY THEN LET GO
- SIT UNDER A TREE AND RELAX
- HAVE A WARM BATH
- SCRIBBLE OR DOODLE TO SOME RELAXING MUSIC
- LISTEN TO RELAXATION MUSIC
- IMAGINE YOU ARE IN A CALM AND RELAXING STATE
- READ A BOOK OR MAGAZINE
- DRINK A CUP OF TEA SLOWLY
- GIVE YOURSELF A FOOT RUB
- TAKE A SOCIAL MEDIA BREAK
- TAKE 5 DEEP BREATHS
- STOP AND LISTEN TO THE BIRDS
- STROKE A PET OR FRIEND'S PET
- DROP YOUR SHOULDERS

CHAMBER OF STRESS MANAGEMENT

"Stress is caused by being here and wanting to be there." *- Eckhart Tolle*

CHAMBER OF STRESS MANAGEMENT

Close your eyes, breathe in slowly, release your shoulders and relax. Walk through the corridors of your mind until you come to the Chamber of Stress Management. Find the correct key, turn the lock, open the door and step inside.

Stand in the middle of the chamber and notice you are surrounded by smoke. You cannot see the walls of the chamber, you can't even see your own body. The smog of stress and anxiety is swirling around you. It is so overwhelming that for the moment you are not able to see past it. Stand still and allow yourself to feel grounded. Feel your whole body and picture it sinking into the floor of the chamber. You feel stable and grounded.

Take in a deep breath and breathe all the way out slowly and steadily. Breathe in and breathe out. Send this breath all the way down to your feet, making you feel anchored to the floor. You may not be able to see your feet but you can feel them. Feel the floor of the chamber with your feet and trust. Take in a deep breath and gently breathe out, feeling the support of the floor beneath your feet. You are safe; you are secure. You notice that the more still and secure you become, the more the smoke of stress and anxiety is thinning and dissipating. Take another breath and breathe out. Notice where your thoughts are now. Allow the thoughts simply to be. Give them space to be acknowledged and heard. Once you become aware of these thoughts, you may find them gently softening and having less of a hold over you. As you continue to remain anchored, you may notice the smoke of stress and anxiety slowly shifting a little more.

To your right is an oxygen mask. Place it over your nose and take in a deep breath. Notice how cool and fresh the oxygen is. Breathe in and feel. Breathe out and let go. Breathe in and feel. Breathe out and let go. Feel the oxygen filling every cell in your body. Breathe deeply.

Feel the smog of stress gently lifting away from you. Notice as it moves away that you continue to stay grounded. You are in control again. You can now see the difference between you and the smog. You notice that you are separate from it. You are not the stress and anxiety. You are separate from

it. Continue to breathe in and out, knowing that you are safe. The stress is slipping away from you. You feel centred and calm.
As the clouds disappear, you notice a screen in front of you. You see an image of yourself in 3D. The image has stress sensors that detect areas of stress and tension in your body and mind. As you look at the image, notice which areas show that you are more vulnerable to stress. You might see them lighting up or flashing red like an alarm. There is a grid with a number of icons. Where do you feel most stress? Can you pinpoint the exact spots?

Around the screen are calming images such as a waterfall, floating clouds, ice cubes melting, trees swaying gently. Choose an image and place the image in the area of tension you feel the most. For example, you may place the image of the waterfall on your shoulders or an ice cube on your stomach. Hold on to the image as it rests on your body and focus on it closely. Notice any changes. Notice how your body starts to release all tension gently and naturally.

You can spend some time experimenting with the stress sensors and calm images until you have brought yourself back into a state of comfort and ease.

When you are ready to leave the chamber, move towards the door and outside into the corridor, knowing you can return to the Chamber of Stress-Management whenever you like.

"I am relaxed; I am relaxed."

Write or draw how you feel in your **CHAMBER OF STRESS MANAGEMENT**

QUESTIONS TO ASK YOURSELF:

What are my stress triggers?

What can I do to manage my stress?

Where do I feel stress in my body?

ACTION:

Do some form of physical exercise for ten minutes a day.

STRESS MANAGEMENT LOG

Date	Why I felt stressed	How I managed the stress

CHAMBER OF RELAXATION

"Tension is who you think you should be. Relaxation is who you are."

- Chinese Proverb

CHAMBER OF RELAXATION

Close your eyes, breathe in slowly, release your shoulders and relax. Walk through the corridors of your mind until you come to the Chamber of Relaxation. Find the correct key, turn the lock, open the door and step inside.

In the middle of the Chamber, you notice a pod. You can sit or lie in the pod and it will take you into a state of deep relaxation. Step inside and close the door and settle in. There are three dials. The first will identify where you are tense, the second will activate the massage mode and the third will take you into a state of deep mind and body relaxation.

Press the first dial and notice your body is being scanned for areas of tension. Follow the scanner and notice the places that feel tense and tight in your body. Breathe in and out slowly as you just observe where you feel tight. The scanner moves over your shoulders, neck, chest and stomach. Notice the sensations of tension and the varying degrees of tension. Do some areas feel tighter than others?

Now press the second dial and special mechanical massage arms extend out towards you. Feel them as they move to the areas of tension helping you release any tightness in your body. Feel the arms pummeling and kneading and unknotting the areas of tension.

Now, press the third dial. You hear some calming sounds or music coming from the pod and the lights dim as it goes into deep relaxation mode. Feel yourself becoming calm and relaxed. Take in a deep breath and breathe all the way out. As you stay there, feel your mind becoming still and quiet. Notice the parts of your body that are in contact with the pod. Feel your back, your hips and your feet relaxing into the pod.

Spend a few moments relaxing the parts of your body that feel tight. Relax your shoulders, relax your neck, relax your jaw and throat. Let everything around you fade into the background as you concentrate on your body. Spend some time letting thoughts of the past and the future fade as you stay present and aware. Stay focused and aware, in the present moment, this moment. Take in a deep breath and breathe out slowly and gently. Notice how the air moves in and out of your body.

As you lie there, you notice how warm you feel. Your muscles feel warm and relaxed. You feel your whole body relaxing and sinking into the pod.

Feel your right hand relaxing. Your right hand is heavy and relaxed. Your right arm is now sinking and becoming heavy and relaxed. Feel your left hand sinking. It is heavy and relaxed. Feel your left arm sinking. Your left arm is heavy and relaxed. Feel your right foot. Your right foot is sinking. It is heavy and relaxed. Feel your right leg sinking. Your right leg is heavy and relaxed. Feel your left foot sinking into the pod beneath you. Your left foot is heavy and relaxed. Feel your left leg softening into the floor of the pod. Your left leg is heavy and relaxed.

Feel your stomach softening and sinking. Your stomach is heavy and relaxed. Take in a deep breath and breathe out, relaxing your stomach. Feel your lower back sinking into the floor of the pod. Your lower back is heavy and relaxed. Take in a deep breath and breathe out, relaxing your lower back. Feel your whole spine becoming relaxed. Feel your shoulders. Your shoulders are sinking and becoming heavy and relaxed. Take in a deep breath and breathe out, relaxing your shoulders. Feel your neck. Your neck is sinking and becoming heavy and relaxed. Take in a deep breath and breathe out, relaxing your neck. Feel your head. Your head is sinking into the pod and becoming heavy and relaxed. Feel your face relaxing and sinking. Relax the your forehead, your right eyebrow, your left eyebrow, your right eye, your left eye, your right cheek, your left cheek, your right ear, your left ear, your right nostril, your left nostril, your upper lip, your lower lip, and your chin. Take a deep breath in and breathe out, relaxing your head as it sinks into the pod.

Stay there for a while, breathing deeply and enjoying the feeling of softness and deep relaxation.

When you are ready, step out of the pod and move towards the door of the Chamber, keeping this deep feeling of relaxation with you.

"I let go and relax; I let go and relax."

Write or draw how you feel in your **CHAMBER OF RELAXATION**

QUESTIONS TO ASK YOURSELF:

What does relaxed mean to me?

What activities can I do to help me feel relaxed?

How can I tell when I'm relaxed?

ACTION:

Make a list of things that make you feel relaxed and aim to do at least one each day.

MINDFUL COLORING

When you feel you need to relax, take time out to color in the image below.

CHAMBER OF SLEEP

"Sleep is the best meditation."

- Dalai Lama

CHAMBER OF SLEEP

Close your eyes, breathe in slowly, release your shoulders and relax. Walk through the corridors of your mind until you come to the Chamber of sleep. Find the correct key, turn the lock, open the door and step inside.

In the chamber is a bed. Everything here has been designed to help you experience optimal sleep and wake up rested and recharged. The bed is surrounded by a number of levers and buttons to ensure you get a personalised experience. Press a button to choose your mattress. You may prefer a hard, supportive mattress or you may prefer a soft one that you can sink into. Press a button to choose the temperature. Would you like it to be cool or heated? Press a button to choose your pillow preference. You can choose a soft feather pillow, or a memory foam pillow, a thin or thick pillow... Which would you like? Press a button to choose the sheets, blankets and duvet. You can opt for a light feather quilt or a warm wooly blanket or soft silk sheets or even a weighted blanket. Which do you choose?

At the foot of the bed is a window. You can choose what you would like to look out on. Press a button to choose some warm sunshine flooding through the window, or the night sky, a relaxing sea or lake scene. There is even a button to close the curtains or blinds. You decide.

You can even press a button to raise or lower the bed or just raise or lower your head or feet. Get into bed and adjust it accordingly to choose your favourite sleeping position. Play around with the buttons to find your perfect combination.

There is also a button for sound by the side of the bed. You can choose what type of sounds you would like to listen to. Spend some time trying out all the different sounds. Try nature, sea waves, rain forest, wind, birdsong, classical music, soft music, gentle singing, drumming or white noise.

You then notice an aromatherapy button. Choose whatever scent you like. Lavender can help with deep sleep, Neroli orange is very calming and lemon helps release tension. Which scent would you like? Take in three deep breaths and enjoy the beautiful natural scent. Above you is a switch to choose the lighting. You can opt for a calming green or blue light, warming red or pink light, fairy lights or a blackout. You can even use the ceiling projector and choose to project a scene such as starlight, underwater, moving clouds or trees in the breeze.

Beside you is a table with a glass or cup. Inside is a cool or warming bedtime drink. What would you like to drink before you sleep?

Once you are perfectly settled in the bed, lie down and feel yourself relaxing. Take a deep breath and smell your chosen scent. Breathe out as slowly and steadily as you can. Breathe in; breathe out. As you breathe, you feel your eyes wanting to close. You try to keep them open, but the desire and need to close them is overwhelming. Breathe in, breathe out, breathe in, breathe out. Feel every muscle in your body giving way and allowing you to slip into a restful sleep. Continue to breathe in and out and feel yourself sinking further and further, more and more deeply into sleep.

"I allow myself to rest; I allow myself to rest."

Write or draw how you feel in your **CHAMBER OF SLEEP**

QUESTIONS TO ASK YOURSELF:

What helps me sleep?

What stops me sleeping?

What do I need to do to improve my sleep?

ACTION:

Create an evening routine that helps you sleep.

MY SLEEP TRACKER

Choose a color for each square in the key. Use this chart to track your sleep every night for a year. See how many good nights sleep you have had!

	J	F	M	A	M	J	J	A	S	O	N	D
1												
15												
30												

Key

- ☐ Great Nights Sleep
  9 hours +
- ☐ Good Nights Sleep
  7 - 9 Hours
- ☐ Average Nights Sleep
  6 - 7 Hours
- ☐ Bad Nights Sleep
  Under 6 Hours
- ☐ Insomnia
  No Sleep

CHAMBER OF EMOTIONS

"Your emotions make you human. Even the unpleasant ones have a purpose. Don't lock them away. If you ignore them, they just get louder and angrier." - Sabaa Tahir

CHAMBER OF EMOTIONS

Close your eyes, breathe in slowly, release your shoulders and relax. Walk through the corridors of your mind until you come to the Chamber of Emotions. Find the correct key, turn the lock, open the door and step inside.

Stand in the middle of a circular room and turn around slowly. You notice a variety of colored buttons on the wall. Each button is a different feeling. Any of these buttons can be activated at any time during your day. Sometimes two or more feelings can be activated simultaneously. When this happens, you can sometimes feel confused and find it hard to unravel what you are feeling.

In the middle of the chamber is a platform. Step up on to the platform and place your hands on your stomach. This area gives you easy access to your feelings. Take a moment, breathe in and out slowly and notice. Notice how you feel right now. You may be having one or more feelings. Continue to breathe deeply all the way into your stomach. Breathe in, breathe out; breathe in, breathe out. Do you notice any other feelings starting to bubble up inside? You may get a sense of a feeling or see a color, word, memory or you may identify a sensation in your body. Can you name that feeling or feelings?

As you stand in the Chamber of Emotions, simply allow yourself to experience those feelings. Breathe in and out deeply and establish a slow and steady breathing pattern. Allow the feelings to come to the surface.

This is a place where all feelings are welcome. You don't need to hide anything. Instead, allow all parts of you to show themselves freely. Invite any feeling in and give it full permission to be there, knowing you are safe and secure. Breathe in and out slowly, letting the sensations flow through your body. As your feelings are activated, you may notice one or more of the colored buttons lighting up in the chamber.

Continue to breathe into the feeling. Let any thoughts, emotions and memories bubble up. Give yourself the rare opportunity to feel them fully. Give the feelings space. Welcome all sensations and notice any micro changes from second to second.

Once you feel your way inside your own feeling, you may notice that it doesn't have so much hold over you or you may view it differently. You may even see that all feelings have their own shape and pattern and are beautiful in their own way as they make you who you are. Continue to allow the feelings to flow through you.

You may also notice that, as you are experiencing these feelings, the buttons are lighting up in a colorful symphony. Gradually, as you practise, you may start to feel that you are the observer of your feelings and you notice that you don't have to be consumed by them, but can create a little gap between you and the feelings. This will help you feel more comfortable with the range of feelings you experience each day.

When you are ready, step off the platform and towards the door and out of the chamber of feelings, knowing that you have gained more understanding and acceptance of your incredible library of feelings. Every feeling is acceptable, natural and normal. You can love and appreciate all of them, whether they are difficult or pleasant feelings.

"I allow all my feelings; I allow all my feelings."

Write or draw how you feel in your **CHAMBER OF EMOTIONS**

QUESTIONS TO ASK YOURSELF:

Where do I feel anger in my body?

Where do I feel fear in my body?

Where do I feel sadness in my body?

Where do I feel happiness in my body?

ACTION:

Write yourself a Happiness prescription and list actions you can do to help you feel happier.

MY INTERNAL WEATHER REPORT

How are you feeling?
Stop for a moment, stay still and take an internal weather report.
Write the date in each box which describes your feeling best

Sunny and happy	Outbreak of rain	Frosty	Thunder most likely	Blustery	Calm	Dense fog and depression	Fine and fair	Blizzard	Scattered clouds	Intermittent rain	Flood Warnings	Clear and relaxed	Warm front

CHAMBER OF CONFIDENCE

"The most beautiful thing you can wear is confidence."

- Blake Lively

CHAMBER OF CONFIDENCE

Close your eyes, breathe in slowly, release your shoulders and relax. Walk through the corridors of your mind until you come to the Chamber of Confidence. Find the correct key, turn the lock, open the door and step inside.

The Chamber of Confidence is a place dedicated to helping you develop your confidence and help you feel better about yourself. In this chamber, you will find a number of confidence tricks and techniques you can trial to help you feel more confident and self-assured.

On one wall of the chamber is a touch screen with three buttons with the words; Be Curious Trick, Talking Trick and Color Cheat.

Press the Be Curious Trick. This can help open your mind to new ways of confident thinking. You simply ask questions, relax, breathe and let your mind find the answers. By asking questions, you are opening yourself up to new answers and possibilities. Ask questions such as: 'How can I be more confident?' Stop and breathe and allow your mind to find the answers. You may see images or words or you may get a feeling. Ask another question: 'What would it be like to feel more confident?' Stay still and allow the answers to bubble up in your mind. You may even like to write or type up the answers on your screen in front of you. You could even use the screen to doodle and draw your answers. 'What do I need to think to become more confident?' 'What do I need to do to become more confident?' 'Who do I know who is confident?' Sit with each question and try to make the answer as long as possible.

Now, try another button on the screen. Press the Talking Trick. Imagine you are standing in a circle surrounded by a group of people who believe in you and want the best for you. They could be real or imaginary people. Take in a deep breath and feel as if you are breathing in confidence. Do this three times and feel the feeling of confidence tingle all over your body. Now, repeat positive words and statements as they watch and cheer you on. Repeat each affirmation slowly and feel the words going right into your mind and body. Feel as if your cells are soaking up each statement and each word. Feel yourself believing each word. Repeat 'I am good enough, I am really good enough, I am OK. I really am OK, I am unique. There is no-one quite like me; I am self-reliant. I am courageous. I believe in myself. I have the power to change; I believe I can. I can do whatever I set my mind to.' Feel your supporters there believing in you.

Now, take a moment to note how you feel in your body and mind at this very moment. When you are ready, press the Color Cheat button. There is a color chart in front of you. Choose a color from the chart that symbolises confidence to you. filling your body filling you with confidence. You are going to imagine that color. Feel a colored laser light beaming from the bottom of your feet, rising slowly through your body. Feel the light coming up through your legs, your spine, neck and out through the top of your head. As the light moves up through you, you feel your are gently elongating. It is almost as if the feeling of confidence is stretching your spinal column. Notice how each vertebrae is slowly being separated by this beautiful column of light. Feel light in the space between each vertebra. You feel the column of light is slowly spreading throughout your body. It is moving out in front of you, behind you, to both sides of you, then above and below you. You are now standing in your own orb of light. It moves with you. The light of confidence is part of you. Wherever you go, you take the light of confidence with you. This is true confidence, not a fake confidence but a confidence that is generated from your inner being. It is authentic inner confidence.

When you are feeling more confident, walk towards the door of the chamber and step outside, knowing you can return briefly or for longer whenever you need to top up your confidence levels.

"I am confident; I am confident."

Write or draw how you feel in your **CHAMBER OF CONFIDENCE**

QUESTIONS TO ASK YOURSELF:

Who do I admire who shows great confidence?

How do they behave and talk?

What skills can I learn from them?

ACTION:

Spend a day walking tall with your shoulders back and notice how this affects your confidence.

MEDALS OF CONFIDENCE

You are amazing! Think about all your best qualities or things you are good at - the things that make **YOU** who you are. Write in the spaces below what you would like to give yourself a medal for.

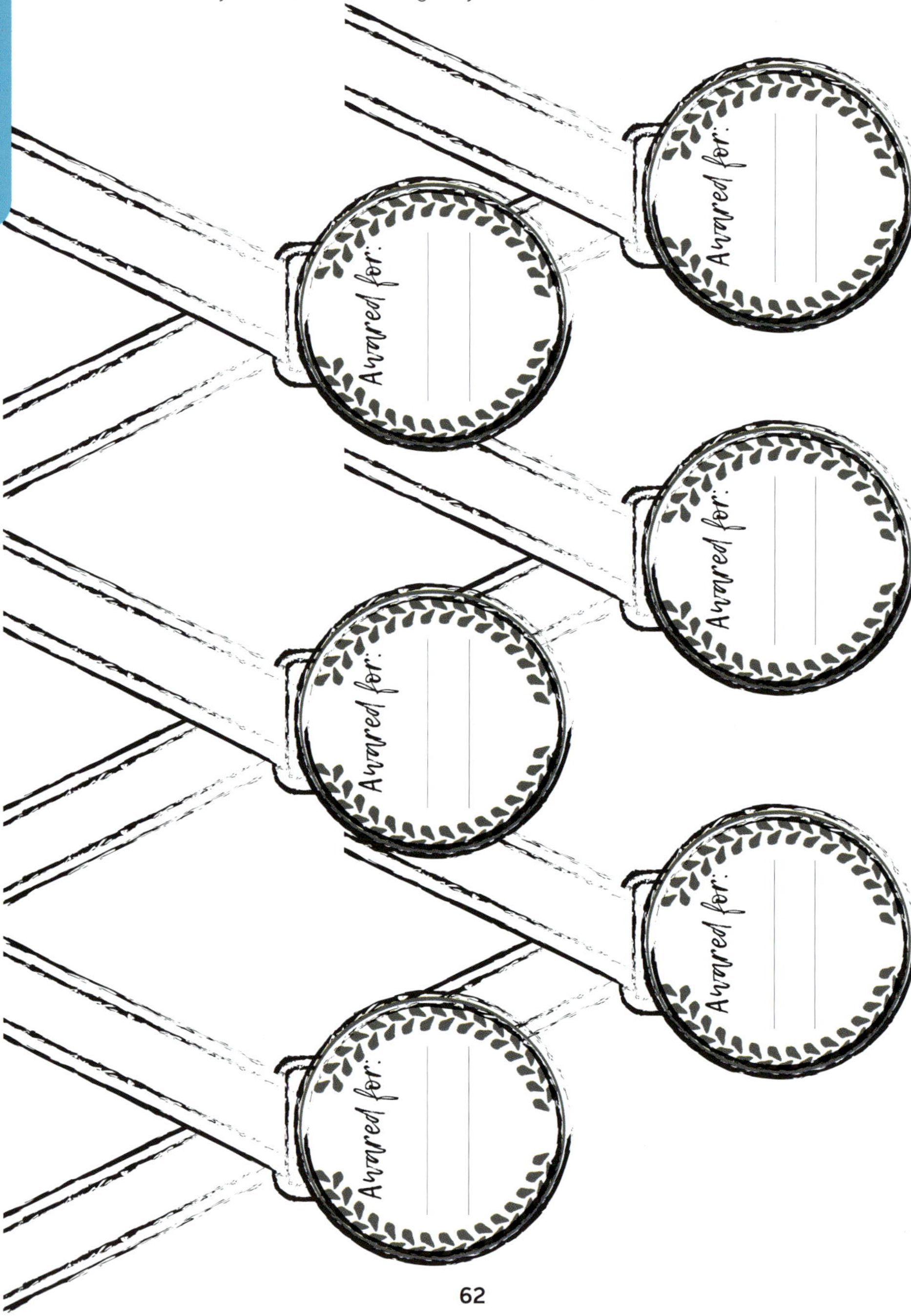

CHAMBER OF LOVE

"What is done in love, is done well." - *Vincent Van Gogh*

CHAMBER OF LOVE

Close your eyes, breathe in slowly, release your shoulders and relax. Walk through the corridors of your mind until you come to the Chamber of Love. Find the correct key, turn the lock, open the door and step inside.

You notice that there is an inner chamber inside. Open the door to the inner chamber. Once inside the inner chamber, you see that there is yet another chamber. Open that door and you find another inner chamber. Keep exploring, going deeper and deeper into the inner chambers until you finally get to the heart of your innermost chamber.

Close the door and sit in the innermost chamber. This is where you let go of the outside world as well as all your thoughts and focus on your own heart space, the very core of you, your truth and the centre of your being. You may like to place your hand on your heart in the middle of your chest. As you sit in the centre of your heart, imagine a soft white, soft pink or golden light shining from your heart lighting up the inner chamber.

Take in a deep breath as you focus fully on your heart. Breathe into your heart and breathe out through your heart. As you breathe out, ask your heart: How do you feel today? What would you like to say? What do you need? Breathe in slowly and breathe out slowly and focus on your heart centre as you sit there in the Chamber of Love. Continue to breathe in and out as you sit still. Focus closely on your heart. Really listen. Be aware. Be present and allow your heart to speak.

Spend a few moments in stillness, allowing your heart to speak and express its feelings. This is a safe space of love for you to quietly feel some deep feelings without judgement. You may not feel anything for a while and that is fine. You may feel some sadness or loneliness. You may feel peace or a sense of contentment. Sit in the chamber of love and just allow any feelings to flow through you and release them all into the chamber.

As you sit, you may feel your heart softening a little or becoming lighter and less burdened. Focus on the warm light in your heart and feel it glow softly. Notice how the light is growing and growing and filling the chamber. Soon the chamber is full of light.

Now send this light of love to those close to you. As you think about your close friends and family, imagine they are being showered in the white, pink or golden light. Breathe in and as you breathe out, feel the light from your heart showering them with love. Imagine their Chamber of Love filling up with the light of love. Breathe in and breathe out and send this love to all the people in your life who you don't know that well but who might also be in need of more love. Shower them with this light of love. Breathe in and breathe out. Feel this beautiful light spreading from your heart to theirs. See their chamber of love lighting up. Now think about all the people who you don't know in the world and send them this beautiful light of love. Breathe in and breathe out and feel them being lit up and showered by this light of love. Feel their Chamber of Love lighting up.

Continue to sit in this beautiful light of love that you have created.

Notice how open-hearted you feel. When you are ready, step out of the inner chamber into the next chamber and fill that chamber with light too. Continue to open the doors to the outer chambers and fill each one of them with light and love.

Take a moment to thank yourself and your heart for creating such a wonderful feeling and step out of the Chamber of Love, knowing that you can return whenever you need to tap back into this feeling of love.

"I am love; I am love."

Write or draw how you feel in your **CHAMBER OF LOVE**

QUESTIONS TO ASK YOURSELF:

What does love mean to me?

What makes me feel loved?

What do I love doing?

ACTION:

Spend a day experimenting with acts of kindness and love. Notice how you feel at the end of the day.

PIECES OF MY HEART

Write down all the things you love in the puzzle pieces below to show all the things that are in your heart.

CHAMBER OF APPRECIATION

"The roots of all goodness lie in the soil of appreciation for goodness."

\- Dalai Lama

CHAMBER OF APPRECIATION

Close your eyes, breathe in slowly, release your shoulders and relax. Walk through the corridors of your mind until you come to the Chamber of Appreciation. Find the correct key, turn the lock, open the door and step inside.

The Chamber of Appreciation is the place you come to when you need to go on a rampage journey of appreciation and fill your mind and body with positivity and energy. Daily visits to this dhamber will help you feel happier, vibrant and more energised.

Sit on the chair in the middle of the chamber and find the augmented reality headset. Position it over your eyes and as it boots up, become aware of your breathing. Feel the softness of your breath coming in and releasing. Spend a few moments watching your breathing. Breathe in, breathe out. Breathe in, breathe out.

Images from your life start to move across the screen. As you see each image, feel grateful and appreciative for that thing or person that is in your life. Even if you wish it were different or you could have a better version, By the simple act of appreciating, you will begin to realise what you do have. As each image comes up on the augmented reality screen, give thanks for it. Breathe in the good feelings and then breathe out. Feel the feelings of appreciation moving through your body.

Begin your rampage journey of appreciation starting with your breath. 'I love and appreciate my breath; it keeps me alive. I appreciate my feet; they hold me up. I appreciate my back; it supports me. I appreciate my senses; they help me experience the world. I love and appreciate my body and look after it with care. I love and appreciate my mind; it allows me to think, reason, remember and create. I love and appreciate my skin; no matter what color it is, it protects me. I love and appreciate every limb as it has a purpose. I love and appreciate my home; it keeps me safe and warm. I love and appreciate food; it nourishes me. I love and appreciate the people who grew the food and who harvested it. I love and appreciate water and hot showers and the people and companies involved in getting water to me. I love and appreciate the nature that is around me - the trees, flowers and insects. I love and appreciate how everything is in perfect balance. I love and appreciate my bed; it helps give me refreshing sleep. I love and appreciate the sun for bringing warmth. I love and appreciate the earth for giving me everything I need to survive. I love and appreciate the air for moving through my body. I love and appreciate all different weathers. I love and appreciate my clothes; they keep me warm and they also enable me to express myself.

I love and appreciate the people who have helped make the clothes. I love and appreciate people in my life for caring and supporting me. I love and appreciate my friends for bringing me happiness and fun times. I love and appreciate my teachers and place of learning. I love and appreciate the pets and animals in my life. I love and appreciate my personality and the parts of me that make me unique and special. I love and appreciate bikes, cars, buses and trains that enable me to get to where I need to be. I love and appreciate the technology that entertains and educates me. I love and appreciate all the good things in my life that bring me joy. I also love and appreciate all the things that are not so good but help me to learn and also help me to appreciate what is good.

When you are ready, walk towards the door of the chamber and step outside, knowing you can return briefly or for longer periods whenever you need to feel appreciative.

"I love and appreciate my life; I love and appreciate my life."

Write or draw how you feel in your **CHAMBER OF APPRECIATION**

QUESTIONS TO ASK YOURSELF:

What in your life do you appreciate?

How do you feel when you appreciate more?

Who could you show more appreciation to?

ACTION:

Spend the day noticing everything around you and appreciate each moment.

WRITE DOWN ALL THE THINGS, PLACES AND PEOPLE YOU APPRECIATE IN YOUR LIFE.

CHAMBER OF POWER

"You have power of your mind - not outside events. Realize this and you will find strength." - Marcus Aurelius

CHAMBER OF POWER

Close your eyes, breathe in slowly, release your shoulders and relax. Walk through the corridors of your mind until you come to the Chamber of Power. Find the correct key, turn the lock, open the door and step inside.

In the centre of the Chamber of Power is a circle of light on the floor. Step into the circle of power and stand still. Feel your feet pressing into the floor and allow your breathing to slow down. Feel your toes spreading as you become grounded and strong. You notice the soft golden light from the floor is running up through your feet. Breathe in and feel as if you are drawing the light up through your feet and ankles. On the next breath in, feel the light moving up your legs to your knees. Breathe in and feel the light moving up to your hips and breathe out gently. Breathe in again and feel the light moving up to your stomach and chest. Feel the light radiating through your body and breathe out. Breathe in and feel the light moving up into your neck and head. Breathe out softly. Feel the light moving through your body like a scanner. Feel your body tingling with this light.

Feel yourself connected to the ground and the light below you. Feel the power of this light in your body. Notice the energy, the vibrancy, the power. Hold your power. Claim your power. Sense your power. Feel your power. See your power. Touch your power. Be your power. Stay in your power.

As you stand in your power, repeat the words: 'I am powerful. I am strong. I am steady. I am stable. I am secure. I am mighty. I am a force of nature. I am courageous. I am brave. I am resilient. I am stable. I am steady. I am strong. I am powerful. I am powerful. I am powerful.'

Place your hand on or just above your stomach. This is the centre of your power. Breathe in deeply and feel your power and energy growing and spreading. Breathe in power and feel every cell of your body filling with this power. Breathe out power. Breathe in and feel every organ of your body filling with power. Breathe out power. Breathe in power and feel every muscle filling with power. Breathe out power. Breathe power into your whole body. Hold your breath for five counts, holding the power in your chest and breathe out slowly.

Now tap your collar bone with your fingers of one hand. As you firmly tap, repeat: 'I am strong and powerful, I am strong and powerful, I am strong and powerful, I am strong and powerful.'

When you are ready, step out of the chamber, remembering that you can return whenever you need a top-up of power.

"I am powerful; I am powerful."

Write or draw how you feel in your **CHAMBER OF POWER**

QUESTIONS TO ASK YOURSELF:

What makes me feel powerful?

How can I develop my power?

What or who takes away my power?

ACTION:

Choose a color that makes you feel powerful and spend a day immersed in that color. Notice how it makes you feel.

POWER BOOSTERS	POWER DRAINERS	POWER TOOLS
What gives you energy and fills you with inner power and strength? Who boosts your inner power?	What drains your energy and inner power and strength? Who drains your inner power?	What can you do to build your inner power?

CHAMBER OF CHANGE

"If you change the way you look at this, the things you look at change."

- Wayne Dyer

CHAMBER OF CHANGE

Close your eyes, breathe in slowly, release your shoulders and relax. Walk through the corridors of your mind until you come to the Chamber of Change. Find the correct key, turn the lock, open the door and step inside.

In the middle of the Chamber of Change is a booth. Step into the booth and sit down. This is your life booth where you can replay the whole of your life and even watch your future life. Switch it on and watch how your name and date of birth come up on the screen. A video begins showing pictures of you as a baby. As you watch your video reel, notice how many changes there have been in your life. Changes in seasons, changes in day and night, changes in body shape, height and shoe size, changes in age, changes in hair style, changes in clothes, changes in moods, changes in likes and dislikes, changes in friendships, changes in places, changes in activities and changes in happy or upsetting events.

Your whole life has been full of changes, whether you have noticed them or not. Some creep up slowly like changes in age and height and some happen suddenly and you find these hard to adjust to. Amidst all the change, there is one part of you that doesn't change and that is the part that is watching the video, the part that is observing your life, the part of you that never gets older. This is the part of you that you can access when you are still and quiet. Your inner self never changes but learns to adapt to changes. You cannot always control the changes that are happening around you, but you can control how calm and peaceful you feel inside. Watch the video again and notice that it is your inner self watching all these changes in your life video.

Take in a deep breath and notice how you feel. Do you feel more calm and peaceful knowing that your inner self is unaffected by the changes in your body and situations? Do you feel more calm knowing that you don't have to try to control but can let changes happen, knowing that you are safe inside and unharmed by change? The more you can access this inner self, the more you will be able to feel calmer when things are moving and changing around you. Continue to breathe deeply and access this point of inner calm.

You may like to freeze frame the video at a point where you were in a state of anxiety or stress during a change. Be aware of how you felt and what you were thinking. Imagine how you would have felt if you had had access to this inner self of calm. Breathe in and breathe out slowly. Now replay the scene and imagine how much easier it would have been if you had access to this inner calm.

Now press the forward button on the video screen and watch your future life. See yourself getting older, experiencing new situations, meeting different people and living in different places. As you watch, you notice it is all happening around you and not affecting you because your inner space of calm is not affected.

Now, rewind the video and bring it to the present and a situation you find challenging. Watch yourself in the situation on the screen. Continue to breathe in and out deeply as you access the point of calm in your inner space. Watch the changes happening around you.

Be the observer, unaffected and still in your position of inner calm. See how long you can stay in your inner calm remembering to breathe deeply. How do you feel now about the changes that are happening around you? Do you feel different? Do you feel calmer and more in control and ready to handle transitions and changes?

When you are ready, step out of the booth and walk towards the chamber door. As you leave the chamber, remind yourself that your inner calm goes with you wherever you go and you can access it through your breathing.

"I am calm; I am calm."

Write or draw how you feel in your **CHAMBER OF CHANGE**

QUESTIONS TO ASK YOURSELF:

How do I react to change?

What can I do to manage change better?

ACTION:

Change a habit (get out of bed on the other side or brush your teeth with your other hand) and notice how you feel.

CHANGE DETECTOR

✔ ✘

1. .... ☐

2. .... ☐

3. .... ☐

4. .... ☐

5. .... ☐

6. .... ☐

7. .... ☐

8. .... ☐

9. .... ☐

10. .... ☐

Think of 10 things that have changed in your life and tick if they have changed it for the better or cross if they have changed it for the worse.

CHAMBER OF POSITIVITY

"The positive thinker sees the invisible, feels the intangible and achieves the impossible." - Winston Churchill

CHAMBER OF POSITIVITY

Close your eyes, breathe in slowly, release your shoulders and relax. Walk through the corridors of your mind until you come to the Chamber of Positivity. Find the correct key, turn the lock, open the door and step inside.

The whole chamber is filled with a soft yellow light. As soon as you step inside, you feel slightly lighter and happier. Take a seat in the big yellow chair and feel yourself relaxing.

In front of you is a large dial. You can adjust the dial to increase or decrease your inner state of positivity. Sit comfortably on the chair and tune into your current mental state. Notice how you feel. Where is the dial at currently? Is it on zero or a low number, or is it on a high number such as 7 or 8? If you feel you would like to increase your positivity levels a little, turn up the dial one or two notches. As you do so, feel your inner brightness intensifying. Feel yourself getting lighter and lighter, happier and happier.

You notice there is a headpiece to your right. This helps re-wire your brain and turn up your positivity levels by playing positive words. Put the headphones on and listen to the positive vocals spoken over relaxing music. They play directly into your mind. You can choose the music and choose the volume. You also have a remote so that you can press repeat, replay or pause the sound at any time. You are in control.

Listen to the words that come through your headphones: 'You are light. You are positive. You are OK. Everything is good. Everything has happened for a reason. No matter what, you will be OK. You are strong and brave and can do anything. You are positive and in control of your life. You make the right decisions at all times. You are strong and confident. You are positive and good things come to you because you stay positive. You attract positivity. You always see the good in every situation. You always do your best. You are OK and everything will be OK. No matter what happens, you are OK. You will always be OK. Every day in every way, you are getting better and better. You are doing your best and that is the best you can do. You are OK. You are good at so many things. You are unique and valuable. You do whatever you set out to achieve. Believe and you can achieve. You deserve good things. You are perfect just as you are. You are thankful and grateful. You are good enough. Good things happen to you. You are calm and relaxed. You can stay happy and content. You are OK. You are healthy and strong. Everyday you get even stronger. You are always positive. You like being positive.'

How do you feel now? Do you notice any changes in your mind? Do you notice any changes in your body? Can you feel the light of positivity moving through you? Do you feel lighter and brighter? Do you feel in a happier, more cheerful mood?

"I can choose positive thoughts; I can choose positive thoughts."

Write or draw how you feel in your **CHAMBER OF POSITIVITY**

QUESTIONS TO ASK YOURSELF:

What does being positive mean to me?

How can I show positivity to others?

Do I talk positively to myself?

ACTION:

Have a negativity detox day, turning off the news, gossip, social media and negative self-talk.

Positive Outlook

Think about a time from your past, answer the questions below and compare to how your life is now.

IN THE PAST	THE PRESENT
I was...	**I am...**
I didn't have...	**I have..**
I felt...	**I feel...**
I thought...	**I know...**
I wanted...	**I want...**

CHAMBER OF HAPPINESS

"Happiness is not something you postpone for the future; it is something you design for the present." - Jim Rohn

CHAMBER OF HAPPINESS

Close your eyes, breathe in slowly, release your shoulders and relax. Walk through the corridors of your mind until you come to the Chamber of Happiness. Find the correct key, turn the lock, open the door and step inside.

This chamber is a museum of happiness. There are shelves filled with objects and symbols of things and experiences that make you happy. You see brightly-colored objects, gadgets and gizmos. You also see photo frames of people at their happiest. You might be able to see a photo of yourself in a state of happiness. Do you remember where it was taken and where you were? Allow yourself to browse through the happiness objects and artefacts. Feel free to pick up anything you wish. You might see objects from your childhood that gave you great happiness or songs and music tracks that make you want to dance with happiness. You may see smiles, emojis and videos of friends and family members laughing. As you pick up and look at the museum items, notice how you feel. Notice if you feel any tingles or sparks of happiness anywhere in your body or mind.

When you have spent time enjoying the museum artefacts, move further on through the chamber. There, you find a small door to an inner chamber. This is the Chamber of Inner Happiness, the place where things are not needed to bring happiness. This inner chamber is quite small and is often missed and forgotten because most people get lost in the external things that give quick fixes of happiness. Most people are unaware of their Chamber of Inner Happiness. When you access your inner chamber often, you can have a continuous supply of natural happiness that is not reliant on anyone or anything.

Sit in the middle of the small chamber. Unlike the museum of happiness, this room is empty. The lighting is soft and you feel warm and relaxed and a warm breeze flows through the room. You have everything you need. Everything is just right. The temperature is just right, the color scheme and lighting is just right and the soft playing music is just right. Everything is designed to allow you to activate your natural state of inner happiness Breathe in slowly and as you breathe in, feel a gentle breeze of contentment flood through your entire body. Breathe out and feel a wash of contentment move through your mind. Breathe in the words: I am going to be happy. I choose to be happy. I am committed to being happy. My body and mind are quiet and content. I accept my life. Whatever I am looking for, I can find in this inner room of happiness.

Now very gently relax your face. Feel your forehead soften, feel your eyes, resting gently, feel your mouth relax. Slowly feel the corners of your mouth move little by little as you start to smile. Feel your mouth relax as you smile. As you smile, your body sends neural messages that help you feel more and more happy. Feel these positive neurotransmitters surge through your body, helping you to feel happier. Feel-good neurotransmitters such as dopamine, endorphins and serotonin are released as you smile. Continue to hold this smile as you breathe in and out, slowly allowing your whole body to be flooded with feel-good chemicals. Stay still and be mindful of any small changes taking place in your body. See if you can notice the chemicals moving through you. Observe how you feel in your body and mind. Stay still and be mindful, noticing all the changes that have taken place in your body and mind.

"I can choose happiness; I can choose happiness."

Write or draw how you feel in your **CHAMBER OF HAPPINESS**

QUESTIONS TO ASK YOURSELF:

Who makes me happy?

What is happiness?

Would I rather be right or be happy?

How can I make others happy?

ACTION:

Experiment by smiling for as much as you can during the day. See how you feel by the end of the day.

MY RECIPE FOR HAPPINESS

Create a recipe using the steps below to ensure you have a happy day!

First thing in the morning:

Remember to:

Think about:

Before going to bed:

Repeat daily:

CHAMBER OF SUPPORT

Help others achieve their dreams and you will achieve yours. - Les Brown

CHAMBER OF SUPPORT

Close your eyes, breathe in slowly, release your shoulders and relax. Walk through the corridors of your mind until you come to the Chamber of Support. Find the correct key, turn the lock, open the door and step inside.

In the middle of the chamber is a large round globe. This is the earth. Step onto the earth and notice how your whole body weight is supported. Feel your feet sinking into the earth beneath you. Feel yourself completely supported and connected to the earth. Take in a deep breath. Let the breath move up through your feet, legs, stomach and chest and breathe out slowly. Feel yourself connecting to the earth below you. Feel yourself held and supported.

Imagine there is a golden chord coming up through the centre of the earth and hooking onto your feet. Imagine, see, feel or just become aware of the strong pull between yourself and the earth. You may feel yourself being pulled down, sinking or softening into the core of the earth or you may feel a buzz of energy between yourself and the earth. What do you feel? Can you feel the connection?

Once you feel the connection between yourself and the earth, you may start to feel more supported for the earth is your primary support structure. The earth is here to support you but we often forget this and so feel unsupported. Feel yourself being anchored and supported by the earth.

As you notice how you are supported by the earth, you start to reflect on how everything in nature is here to support you. The air supports you by giving you oxygen. and life force. Take a moment to breathe in fresh oxygen. The sun supports you with light and warmth, the night supports your body's natural rhythm for sleep. Take a moment to appreciate the warmth of the sun on your body and the light around. The oceans and rivers support you by giving you water and the animals and plants support you by giving you food. Take some moment to appreciate how you are supported by the earth and the elements.

In the middle of the globe is a chair. Sit down and feel how it is holding you. Notice how you are supported. Let go and allow your body to be supported. Feel how the chair is holding and supporting you. If there are cushions on the chair, notice how they are supporting you. Take a moment to notice the clothes you are wearing and how they are supporting you by protecting your body and keeping you warm.

As you sit, imagine all the people in your life who support you in some way. Imagine your family and friends standing around you and think about how they support you by listening, sharing, caring and giving you what you need. They might not always be there when you want them, but you know that everyone is trying their best in life. You can imagine them putting their hands on your back and shoulders and you are leaning into them and taking their support.

Now imagine a special supportive person in your life: a champion or mentor who really has your back. They may be real or imaginary. Imagine them facing you and telling you that you have everything you need to be a success. They completely believe in you and will always be there when things get tough. Your champion is completely focused on you and is only focused on helping you be the best you can be. They are always positive and enthusiastic and completely un-judgmental. They believe in your strengths and are excited to see you grow and develop. Your champions always give you constructive feedback and fill you with confidence and self-belief.

Whenever you need support, you know you can come back to the Chamber of Support and feel connected to the earth and talk to your mentor, share problems as well as successes. Make a commitment to return often to check in with your mentor.

When you are ready, get up from the chair and step off the globe in the centre of the chamber and walk towards the door. Just before you leave, your mentor gives you a small gift in the shape of a symbol. This is to remind you of the chamber and also of your support structures.

"I am supported; I am supported."

Write or draw how you feel in your **CHAMBER OF SUPPORT**

QUESTIONS TO ASK YOURSELF:

Who are my supports?

Who do I support?

Who can I support more?

ACTION:

Take a problem and imagine how your favourite hero would solve it. You could choose a fictional hero or superhero or a person you admire and look up to.

MY TEAM OF SUPPORTERS

Write down the name of all the people in your life who look out for you and support you.

CHAMBER OF GRATITUDE

"Be thankful for what you have; you'll end up having more. If you concentrate on what you don't have, you will never, ever have enough." - Oprah Winfrey

CHAMBER OF GRATITUDE

Close your eyes, breathe in slowly, release your shoulders and relax. Walk through the corridors of your mind until you come to the Chamber of Gratitude. Find the correct key, turn the lock, open the door and step inside.

Walk around the chamber and notice that at one end there is a counter with a screen. Step towards the counter and you see number of electronic signs with positive slogans.

'Gratitude is the best attitude.'
'Begin everyday with a grateful heart.'
'The secret to having it all is knowing you already do.'
'Gratitude turns life into gold.'

Just watching the brightly-coloured signs flash before your eyes seems to have a positive effect on your state of mind.

You notice on the counter there is a card reader and microphone. There is also a card with your name on it. With this card, you can deposit words and feelings of gratitude into your inner bank. Doing this adds to your inner wealth and happiness.

To make a deposit, you can simply make a statement of gratitude into the microphone or you can hold the card on the reader and think or feel grateful. These are like credits which are added to your account. The more you can appreciate every little thing in life, the greater your inner reserves of strength and happiness will be.

Stand at the counter and prepare to make a deposit into the bank. Think of everything that you are grateful for in your life and mentally speak your feelings into the microphone and watch as your credits increase.

Here are some statements you could make:
'I am grateful for my body. I am grateful for my mind. I am grateful for food and water. I am grateful for family and friends. I am grateful for my home. I am grateful for my life. I am grateful for the sunshine and the air I breathe. I am grateful for the rain. I am grateful for the earth. I am grateful for

learning new things. I am grateful for my bed. I am grateful for rest
Take a deep breath in and breathe out slowly. Breathe in, breathe out. Breathe in and say, 'I am grateful'. Breathe out and say, 'I am grateful'.

Notice how your credit score increases.

Now stand still and place your card on the reader and feel intensely grateful for your body and everything that it does for you. Feel grateful for your mind and your capacity to think, learn, remember and reason. Feel grateful for food and water and think about how it nourishes you and keeps you well. Feel grateful for family and friends and think about how they support you, care for you, love you, laugh with you and make your life easier. Some may make life feel more difficult at times, but feel grateful for what they teach you. Feel grateful for your home. Think or say how grateful you are for your life and how you are able to contribute and make a difference in the world. Feel grateful for the sunshine and rain. Feel grateful for the air you breathe. Take in a deep breath of fresh air and feel grateful for being alive and well. Feel grateful for the earth and think about how it supports you. Feel grateful for what you are learning in life. Feel grateful for your bed and your rest and sleep. Take a deep breath in and breathe out slowly. Breathe in, breathe out. Notice how your credit score has increased.

When you are ready, leave the Chamber of Gratitude, taking your card with you, making a note to visit often to continue to make gratitude deposits and add to your inner wealth account. You may like to read the slogans on the screen on your way out, just to remind you to continue to be grateful at all times.

Remember to repeat your gratitude statements often.

"I am grateful for what I have; I am grateful for what I have."

Write or draw how you feel in your **CHAMBER OF GRATITUDE**

QUESTIONS TO ASK YOURSELF:

What am I grateful for?

Who am I grateful to?

How can I show my gratitude to others more often?

ACTION:

Create a gratitude collage, finding pictures of all the things you are grateful for in your life.

Gratitude List

Make a list of all the things you are grateful for.

CHAMBER OF CHOICES

"It is our choices that show what we truly are, far more than our abilities."

- J.K. Rowling

CHAMBER OF CHOICES

Close your eyes, breathe in slowly, release your shoulders and relax. Walk through the corridors of your mind until you come to the Chamber of Choices. Find the correct key, turn the lock, open the door and step inside.

Inside the Chamber of Choices is another corridor with two doors side by side. There is a blue door and a red door. These are the Doors of Choice. Before you choose which door to open, think about a situation in your life that you would like to solve. Do you have to make a choice? It might be a life choice or a moral choice, a life-style choice or an ethical choice. You may need to make a choice between two possibilities, people or things. What is your dilemma? Both doors are ready for you to open. Open the blue door on the left. Behind the blue door is the outcome of one of your choices. Step into the chamber and see yourself having acted out your choice. What are you doing? Are you happy? Who is with you? Do they look happy? How do you feel being here? Stay still and get a real sense of the outcome of your choice. When you are ready, step out of the chamber and back to the corridor and close the blue door firmly behind you.

Now open the red door on the right. Behind the red door is the outcome of another choice. Step into the chamber and see yourself having acted out your choice. What are you doing? Are you happy? Who is with you? Do they look happy? How do you feel being here? Stay still and get a real sense of the outcome of your choice. When you are ready, step out of the chamber and back to the corridor and close the red door firmly behind you.

Stand in front of the two doors and think about how you feel. Take in a deep breath and notice the feelings in your body. Notice the difference in how you felt when you went into each chamber. Did one give you a better feeling? Did you feel happier or relieved or more alive? Did you feel an inner sense of peace and security? Did you feel more empowered in one? Do you have a better sense now of which is the right choice for you? It might not be instant and you may need to go back through the two doors again to get a sense of which is the right choice, knowing that you can always learn from mistakes as even 'wrong' choices can lead you to the right places.

When you are ready, walk along the corridors of your mind, take a deep breath and open your eyes.

"I trust my choices; I trust my choices."

Write or draw how you feel in your **CHAMBER OF CHOICES**

QUESTIONS TO ASK YOURSELF:

Will I regret my choice?

Who am I really doing this for?

Will I like myself after making this choice?

Will this choice bring me peace and happiness?

ACTION:

Write down a list of all the positive and negative emotions that come up when you are?

DECISION MAKING

Think of a decision you have to make, write the pros and cons for this decision

PROS	CONS

CHAMBER OF BOUNDARIES

"Boundaries define us. They define what is me and what is not me. A boundary shows me where I end and someone else begins, leading me to sense of ownership. Knowing what I am to own and take responsibility for gives me freedom."

- Henry Cloud

CHAMBER OF BOUNDARIES

Close your eyes, breathe in slowly, release your shoulders and relax. Walk through the corridors of your mind until you come to the Chamber of Boundaries. Find the correct key, turn the lock, open the door and step inside.

The Chamber of Boundaries is a place you can come to help get more in touch with your body and learn how to read its internal signs and signals so you can create stronger boundaries to protect yourself.

Sit on comfortable sofa and feel your body relaxing into the plump cushions. Take a couple of deep breaths in and out and become aware of your body from the inside. Notice how you feel in your body right here and right now. How does your stomach feel? How does your throat feel? How does your heart feel?

As you sit on the sofa, a simple presentation appears with words and diagrams on the screen in front of you. It shows you how to protect yourself. Your body has a clever system that helps keep you safe, remain in your power and helps you keep your inner peace.

When boundaries are weak and you don't say 'NO', your internal security system goes down which can affect your nervous system making you feel anxious or depressed.

Your body's internal security warning system is excellent. When you feel unsafe or uneasy in a situation or when you are with someone, you may feel a tightness in your stomach or throat. It is easy to ignore this internal security system. But when you do, little by little, you give away your power.

You can learn to test and monitor your security system by getting in tune with your body and accessing the three alarm bells in the stomach, chest and throat. Testing these alarms often will help you be more in touch with your body.

You can test out your system by imagining people and situations and check in with your three alarms - stomach, heart and throat - and notice their reaction. You may notice your heart beats more quickly when you see one person or you feel tight in your throat as if you want to shout or scream at someone. Your body picks up everything. Continue to notice; continue to feel; continue to be aware; continue to focus on your alarm system.

Now take in a deep breath and breathe out slowly and imagine you are saying 'NO'. 'No' to the person or situation that was flashing up on the screen. Notice how that feels in your body now. Notice the changes. You can practise saying 'No' to everyone and everything you want to test your boundaries out with. Notice how you feel. Notice how your power is returning and with each 'No' you are feeling more and more in control and better about yourself. Notice how you are owning your space, your body, your feelings, your power and your boundaries.

Before you leave the chamber, you notice there is a marker pen. Take the marker pen and stand in an empty part of the chamber. Draw a circle around you to mark where you would like your boundary to be. Stand in your circle of power and feel safe and secure. Breathe in and breathe out. Notice how your heart beat and breathing are calm as you stand in your circle. Now focus on your three internal alarms. Place your hand on your throat, and notice how it feels. Place your hand on your chest and notice how that feels. Place your hand on your stomach and notice how that feels. This is your optimum position and so you have something to compare with next time your alarm bells are ringing.

When you feel your boundaries are strong, step out of the circle towards the door, remembering to check in with your inner alarm system regularly.

"I can tune into what feels right for me; I can tune into what feels right for me."

Write or draw how you feel in your **CHAMBER OF BOUNDARIES**

QUESTIONS TO ASK YOURSELF:

What are my boundaries?

Who do I need to set up better boundaries with?

ACTION:

Give yourself permission to set boundaries and put your feelings first. Make a list of the boundaries you would like to set.

MY BOUNDARIES

What do I want to say **YES** to?

What do I want to say **NO** to?

CHAMBER OF SOLUTIONS

"Every problem has in it the seeds of its own solution. If you don't have any problems, you don't get any seeds."

- Norman Vincent Peale

CHAMBER OF SOLUTIONS

Close your eyes, breathe in slowly, release your shoulders and relax. Walk through the corridors of your mind until you come to the Chamber of Solutions. Find the correct key, turn the lock, open the door and step inside.

Inside the Chamber of Solutions you notice a conveyor belt running all around the chamber. On the conveyor belt is the solution to every problem you could possibly have. Watch as an array of solutions move past you slowly. Notice the variety of weird and wonderful objects. You may not think that one of these strange objects can give you an answer, but just allow them to drift past your eyes and your mind. Let the shapes, colors and textures of the objects spark an idea.

Take some time to identify what problem you would like to find the solution to. Take in a deep breath and breathe out, describing the problem three times. If the problem is a person or situation, visualise it on a screen in front of you. If it is a feeling, notice where it is in your body. Notice how your body is feeling and notice how your mind is feeling. Do you feel any areas of tightness and resistance in your body or mind? Notice what chemical reactions are happening in your body when you think of a problem.

Now focus on the moving conveyor belt. What objects are moving past on your conveyor belt? What supportive tools can you see? You know that the solution to your problem is in one of these tools. You just have to choose the right one. Which tool do you need right now? Do you need glasses to help give a new perspective? Or would you like mental fan to create some inner air conditioning and help you cool down? Maybe you need a balloon to tie the problem to and let it go? A torch to shine some light on the problem or paint and brushes to use your creativity? You could choose a picture frame or mirror to reframe the problem or help you see it from a different angle. You could choose a suitcase to pack up the problem or a plant to inspire you to find new ways to grow. What about a cuddly toy or a cushion to help you feel safe and supported?

Once you have chosen an item from the conveyor belt, hold it in your hands and breathe deeply. Breathe in and breathe out, in and out. As you hold the object, notice how it feels in your hands. Notice how warm or cold it is, how flexible or firm, how light or heavy it is. Notice if the object has a smell or sound. Focus completely on the object in your hands. Allow the object to show you the solution that you need. Let your mind go free as the object unravels the problem and finds a creative solution. You may notice how your thoughts are like tendrils moving through your mind finding solutions. Let your mind be free and your thoughts roam. It is in these roaming creatively free flowing moments, that you find clarification, answers and resolutions.

Breathe in and out slowly as you hold the object in your hands. Feel creative ideas and solutions flow through you. Feel yourself coming up with new ways to address your problem. Feel yourself becoming more resilient. Feel your creativity flowing. Feel your energy rising as your determination increases. Feel yourself becoming more understanding and knowledgeable. Feel yourself being more experienced and wise. Feel yourself becoming more relaxed and easy about problems, knowing that you have access to every solution.

When you feel ready, place the object back on the conveyor belt and start to walk out of the chamber, knowing that you can return whenever you need to. You can even return briefly when you are in the middle of a problem and need a quick solution. The solution will always be here, inside.

"Everything I need is within; everything I need is within."

Write or draw how you feel in your **CHAMBER OF SOLUTIONS**

QUESTIONS TO ASK YOURSELF:

What one small change could I make that would make help solve this?

How many solutions can I come up with to solve this?

Who do I know that has overcome a similar problem?

Can I seek support from them?

ACTION:

Take a problem and imagine how your favourite hero would solve it. You could choose a fictional hero or superhero or a person you admire and look up to.

PROBLEM SOLVING

Imagine you are posting on an advice forum about a problem. Write your problem below

PROBLEM

Now imagine you are a different user, responding to the problem you have posted. What advice would you give?

SOLUTION

CHAMBER OF CREATIVITY

"If you hear a voice within you say, 'You cannot paint,' then by all means paint, and that voice will be silenced."

- Vincent Van Gogh

CHAMBER OF CREATIVITY

Close your eyes, breathe in slowly, release your shoulders and relax. Walk through the corridors of your mind until you come to the Chamber of Creativity. Find the correct key, turn the lock, open the door and step inside.

In the middle of the Chamber of Creativity is a large, comfortable sofa or chair. Take a seat and relax. To enable you to access your inner creativity, you need first to feel in a state of calm and comfort. Take in a deep breath and breathe out slowly. Allow your breathing to slow down until you reach a state of calm. Your brain is at its most creative when you feel safe and calm.

Creativity is simply putting something together in a different way to form something new. Everything in this world has been created by someone's mind. Engineers create using Maths and Science. Artists use paint and canvas in different combinations to create art.

Musicians put notes together to create music. Authors put words together in different combinations to create stories, novels and poems and philosophers put thoughts together to create new ideas.

To create something in your mind, you need to have space. So feel yourself breathing into this space. Take time to rest because creativity needs space and rest. Feel yourself breathing into the space. Breathe in and breathe out slowly. Feel yourself letting go of all unwanted thoughts and allowing for new and creative thoughts to enter the chamber. Breathe in and breathe out any feelings that might hamper your creativity. Breathe in slowly and notice new thoughts arising. Breathe in and breathe out.

Focus on the screen in front of you and as you let new thoughts emerge from your mind, you see shapes, colors or symbols appearing on the screen in front of you. Sit back, relax and allow the thoughts, shapes, colors and symbols to flow without expectation or force.

Maybe you only see figures or colors or words. Allow your creative thoughts and ideas move freely as they appear on the screen in front of you. Let your creativity flow like a stream. If you feel nothing is coming, just allow your body to sink deeper into the chair or sofa and relax. There is no need for pressure or force.

To help your creativity, you may like to ask open-ended questions such as "I wonder if..." or "I wonder why...."or 'I wonder how..."

After a while, you may start to make connections between thoughts and shapes. Images, scenes and pictures may emerge in front of you. You may see a mind map developing. Continue to breathe deeply as you allow your brain to continue its creative process. Stay in this relaxed, creative space for as long as you wish. Let the thoughts flow like a river running through you.

When you have finished, stay still and take an inner snapshot of your creation. You can take this away with you to inspire you to create something new.

"I am creative; I am creative."

Write or draw how you feel in your **CHAMBER OF CREATIVITY**

QUESTIONS TO ASK YOURSELF:

What is the best thing I have created?

What new thing would I like to create?

In a hundred years time from now, what would I like to have created?

ACTION:

Spend ten minutes doodling or brainstorming. You can take any object or word or even a world/social problem and see what ideas you can come up with.

MY BRILLIANT IDEAS MIND MAP

MY IDEAS

CHAMBER OF SAFETY

"Safety is not a gadget but a state of mind." - Eleanor Everett

CHAMBER OF SAFETY

Close your eyes, breathe in slowly, release your shoulders and relax. Walk through the corridors of your mind until you come to the Chamber of Safety. Find the correct key, turn the lock, open the door and step inside.

The Chamber of Safety is a large space where you can come and build your own safe space. This safe space is a place you can come to whenever you need to turn inwards and feel some safety and reassurance. It is a private place designed to make you feel completely secure.

What type of safe space would you like to build here? Do you need a large open space or a small cosy space? Why do you need this space? What will its purpose be? You may be an introverted type of person who loses energy from being around people for long periods of time and who needs somewhere to recharge alone. On the other hand, you maybe an extrovert type who gains energy and a buzz from being social and so only need a quieter space to take a short breather.

Once you know what you need and how you are going to use the space, you can think about what type of building you would like. A house? A castle? A room? A circular wall? A box? A dome? A glass house or maybe a bubble? You can create whatever space you wish with whatever materials you like. It could be made out of soft velvety fabrics, brightly coloured timber, recycled or natural materials. Spend time dreaming into creation. Create a space that will make you feel most safe and comfortable. As you build your safe space, feel as if you are breathing calm and peace into the whole area so you are setting the intention for peace and safety.

Make sure you have a door and a window so you can look out on the world and also step out and interact when you wish to and retreat when you need safety and reassurance.

Now your space is created, step inside and breathe in and out slowly. Notice how you feel in your body as soon as you set foot in the space. Can you feel the effect it is having on you? Do you feel safe here? What else do you need to help you feel safe and secure? Is there anyone you would like to bring into your space to help you feel safe?

Once you have created your safe space, you can do what you like there. You can sit or lie down and rest, reflect, dream, sleep, doodle, move, practise your breathing or just be. Simply notice how you feel in your safe space. You can stay here for as long as you wish. The space is yours.

When you are ready to leave, walk out of the Chamber of Safety, knowing it is there for you to return to at any point. You always have the key to this safe space; you always have a place to go to.

"I am safe and protected; I am safe and protected."

Write or draw how you feel in your **CHAMBER OF SAFETY**

QUESTIONS TO ASK YOURSELF:

What makes me feel safe?

What makes me feel unsafe?

Where is my safe place?

ACTION:

Spend some time creating a cosy safe space in your home.

CIRCLE OF SAFETY

Write/draw all the things that make you feel safe inside the circle of safety and write/draw all things that make you feel unsafe outside the circle

After you have done the exercise, ask yourself these questions. What do you notice about your circle of safety? Is there someone you could talk to about it?

CHAMBER OF BELIEFS

"If you think you can do a thing or think you can't do a thing, you're right."

- Henry Ford

CHAMBER OF BELIEFS

Close your eyes, breathe in slowly, release your shoulders and relax. Walk through the corridors of your mind until you come to the Chamber of Beliefs. Find the correct key, turn the lock, open the door and step inside.

Walk into the Chamber of Beliefs and notice how it is like stepping into a complicated computer program. All around you are rows and rows of processors. Inside each processor are millions of switches. This complex computer stores all your thoughts, feelings, emotions, memories and beliefs.

This is the Chamber of Beliefs. In here are all the beliefs you have gathered about yourself from a very early age. These beliefs are so programmed in to your mind that they affect your thoughts, feelings, emotions and memories. Everything you think, do and say is filtered through your belief programme. Your belief program is a list of instructions with a database of memories and instructions that are responsive. It is the inbuilt program that makes you react to people and situations in ways that you might not want to react. Your beliefs drive your behaviour.

Beliefs are statements that you have heard as a child, taken in, accepted and learnt to be true even if they might not be true. Once a belief is programmed into you, you can feel you are locked in a pattern and story and it can be hard to override it until you create a new set of beliefs and upgrade your internal system. Beliefs are messages such as 'I can't do it' or 'I'm not good enough' or 'I'm not attractive'. As a child, you were a sponge and took every word, idea, view, comment, criticism and judgement you heard from others into your computer system without checking its validity. You have now accumulated a collection of beliefs, many of which are not yours and are not good for you.

There is a notice in front of you with step-by-step guidelines on how to change your negative belief programme and feel more content, how to accept yourself more fully and build better habits and relationships.

Take in a deep breath and breathe out slowly. Press the belief key and see a list of all the beliefs you have about yourself come up. What are your main beliefs? What do you think or say about yourself most all of the time? What can you hear ringing in your head?

Choose a belief that you hear yourself saying a lot. Remember to breathe and notice how it makes you feel. Can you remember where you heard it first? Who said it? Where were you? Can you picture the scene on the computer screen in front? Try and gather as much information around it as you can. You might even see visuals on the screen where you can identify how this belief has affected your behaviour.

Next, if you have decided you would like to change the program on this belief, go to the computer, breathe in and turn down the volume control. Breathe in and then dim the brightness on the visuals so the scene has almost disappeared.

Take a pause as you take another breath. You can now decide if you would like to change the belief. If you would like to make a change and upgrade your operating system, first decide if you are willing to take on that belief anymore. Once you have decided, take a deep breath as you replay the scene again. Continue to slow down your breathing as you change the belief by switching the point of view and seeing the scene where you first took on the belief from a completely different angle. You may see it with compassion for yourself as a little child who took on this belief without knowing the consequences. You might also have a better understanding of why the person who instilled this belief in you did so. Do you see their words as the truth now? Or do you see that the words were muddled by the beliefs they themselves took on from a previous generation?

What new beliefs would you like now? Spend some time writing in a new computer program with a new set of beliefs that you would like to live by.

When you are ready, step out of the Chamber of Beliefs, knowing that you can return whenever you want to erase an old belief that has caused you difficulty, upgrade your system and re-boot your operating methods.

"I believe I am enough; I believe I am enough."

Write or draw how you feel in your **CHAMBER OF BELIEFS**

QUESTIONS TO ASK YOURSELF:

What are the beliefs I have about myself?

What is my truth?

Where did I pick these up from?

How can I change my beliefs?

ACTION:

Spend some time thinking about how your beliefs affect your actions and behavior.

MY OLD BELIEFS	MY NEW BELIEFS
Things I used to believe	Things I currently believe

CHAMBER OF ACCEPTANCE

"Be who you are and say what you feel because those who mind don't matter and those who matter don't mind."

- Dr Seuss

CHAMBER OF ACCEPTANCE

Close your eyes, breathe in slowly, release your shoulders and relax. Walk through the corridors of your mind until you come to the Chamber of Acceptance. Find the correct key, turn the lock, open the door and step inside.

The Chamber of Acceptance has been designed to give you everything you need to help you love and accept yourself. If you need anything, you just have to ask and it will appear. You are going to give yourself a full VIP experience as you are the most important person in your life.

Follow the red carpet and you will see the sign to the VIP area. You see a comfortable swing chair and sit down. Feel yourself rocking backwards and forwards as you read the menu card. The menu of experiences is divided into three sections. Starter – Attention; Main – Affection; and Dessert - Affirmation.

Attention, affection and affirmation are the three things everyone needs in order to accept themselves. Often we didn't get all three as children and so it is important now to focus on these three things in order to feel that sense of self-worth and acceptance. A daily dose of all three will help you feel kinder and more loving towards yourself.

Are you ready to be pampered and feel like a VIP from the inside?

For the starter, someone appears opposite you. This could be someone you love dearly or it could be someone you have never met but admire deeply or look up to. Whoever it is, they are sitting in a swing chair opposite you and giving you their full attention as a mentor. They only want what is best for you and they also want to give you their undivided attention in a way that you may never have received before. For the next little while, they will look into your eyes and really see the true you. How does it feel to be completely seen by someone who totally believes in you? Nothing else matters and nothing else exists for you other than you and your mentor. You are both totally present. If you wish, you can say something and they will listen or you can simply enjoy the silence and feeling of being understood.

For this time, there is just you and your mentor, both totally present and completely aware and enjoying the moment. All the focus is on you and what you need. As you receive this attention, your inner confidence and self-belief begins to grow and you feel more accepting of yourself. Feel yourself smiling inside. Stay here for as long as you wish.

When you are ready, you can go onto the main course. This is where you will receive affection. You are about to have a relaxing back and shoulder rub or a head stroke or a hug. You can choose who you would like to give you a massage or hug. Your chosen person only wants the best for you and wants to show you how special you are by giving you a relaxing massage or hug. Feel their hands on your shoulders caring for you and supporting you. As they massage you, all the tightness in your shoulders melts away. As they stroke your forehead lovingly, you feel calm and relaxed. As they hug you, your whole body melts into their loving hug. You feel you are surrounded by love and your body is flooded with endorphins. Stay here for as long as you wish.

When you are ready, you can go on to the dessert course. For dessert, you are treated to a long, cool drink of positive affirmations. A delicious looking drink appears in front of you. Sip through the straw and breathe in through your mouth. As you breathe in, imagine you are breathing in love and acceptance. Breathe in and feel yourself becoming full of self-worth. Say to yourself: 'I am OK just as I am. I am imperfectly perfect. I am enough. I am good enough. I am doing my best. My best is enough. I am enough. I deserve good things. I accept myself and all parts of myself. I am enough; I am enough.' Continue to repeat these affirmations for as long as you wish, all the while enjoying the delicious drink. Notice how you feel.

You are the VIP in your own life. You just have to remember how special you are and treat yourself as a deeply special person.

As you get up to leave the chamber, you hear cheers and a round of applause. Walk out, following the red carpet to the door knowing that you are special, valuable and important.

"I can accept myself just as I am; I can accept myself just as I am."

Write or draw how you feel in your **CHAMBER OF ACCEPTANCE**

QUESTIONS TO ASK YOURSELF:

Am I who I want to be?

How can I accept myself more?

How can I accept others more?

ACTION:

Spend a day being kind and self-accepting. Become aware of how you talk to yourself. Notice how you feel by the end of the day.

MIRROR OF ACCEPTANCE

Write all the things you love about yourself and all things you accept about yourself in the mirror. Write all things you find more difficult to accept about yourself outside the mirror.

CHAMBER OF KINDNESS

"Kindness is the language that the deaf can hear and the blind can see." - Mark Twain

CHAMBER OF KINDNESS

Close your eyes, breathe in slowly, release your shoulders and relax. Walk through the corridors of your mind until you come to the Chamber of Kindness. Find the correct key, turn the lock, open the door and step inside.

The Chamber of Kindness is the place where you come to be nourished and nurtured. It is a place where you feel supported by loving kindness. Just by entering the chamber, you are taking the first step towards being kind to yourself. Take some time to walk around the chamber. There is everything you need here to show yourself kindness. There are jugs of fresh juice and fruit flavoured waters, warm drinks, exercise machines, A hugging machine, A massage chair, a body-listening gadget, a compliments appliance and even a sleep tool. Everything has been set up to enable you to relax and let go.

Sit down in the comfortable chair and pick up the special listening gadget. This gadget allows you to take a moment and really listen to your body and what you need. Do you need rest? Do you need a hug? Do you need to move? Do you need to talk? Do you need to write? Do you need a shoulder rub? Put the headphones on and listen to your breathing and tune in to your whole body and notice what you need. This is the quickest and easiest way to showing kindness to yourself.

If you would like a relaxing massage, pick up the remote and switch to the massage setting. Choose the settings you need to massage the muscles that feel most tight. Feel your body relaxing into the softness of the chair. Feel yourself completely supported as the chair rolls over and kneads your tightest or sorest muscles. Let your breathing slow down and in turn feel yourself slowing down. You feel soft and relaxed.

As you sit in the chair, you can choose a drink of fresh juice, fruit water or a warm drink. Feel the coolness or warmth of the cup on your hands. Take in a deep breath and smell the aroma of the drink. Focus completely on the drink as you take a sip. Feel it slipping down your throat and hydrating and nourishing your body. You can also try the compliments appliance. This machine will give you positive affirmations and compliments which will help send a good feeling all through your mind and body. Press the switch and listen to the succession of compliments and positive statements. "You are enough. You are good enough. You are OK just as you are. You are special.

You are amazing". Stay in the chair listening to the compliments for as long as you need.

If you would like a relaxing massage, pick up the remote and switch to the massage setting. Choose the settings you need to massage the muscles that feel most tight. Feel your body relaxing into the softness of the chair. Feel yourself completely supported as the chair rolls over and kneads your tightest or sorest muscles. Let your breathing slow down and in turn feel yourself slowing down. You feel soft and relaxed.

As you sit in the chair, you can choose a drink of fresh juice, fruit water or a warm drink. Feel the coolness or warmth of the cup on your hands. Take in a deep breath and smell the aroma of the drink. Focus completely on the drink as you take a sip. Feel it slipping down your throat and hydrating and nourishing your body.

You can also try the compliments appliance. This machine will give you positive affirmations and compliments which will help send a good feeling all through your mind and body. Press the switch and listen to the succession of compliments and positive statements. "You are enough. You are good enough. You are OK just as you are. You are special. You are amazing". Stay in the chair listening to the compliments for as long as you need.

You can stay in the chair and read or write or you may like to get up and do some stretching or exercise. You can choose your favourite music and stretch or exercise to the music. As you move, notice how each of your muscles are connected to each other. Feel a sense of gratitude for your body and the movement it allows you. Continue to breathe.

You may like to continue moving and exercising or you may like to have a go on the hugging machine. Step into the machine and the arms are activated. As you are completely engulfed in a soft warm hug, your body begins to relax and release endorphins which make you feel even more relaxed and happy. You can remain on the hugging machine for as long as you wish, noticing how your breathing is softening and heart beat is slowing down.

Once your body is flooded with endorphins, you may like to curl up in a fluffy blanket and just rest or sleep for a while. Feel your body warming up in the blanket, allowing you to drift into the most relaxing restful sleep or daydream.

Continue to dream or sleep for as long as you need. When you are ready, get up feeling relaxed and refreshed. Make a note to revisit the Chamber of Kindness whenever you need a self-kindness boost.

"I am kind to myself and others; I am kind to myself and others."

Write or draw how you feel in your **CHAMBER OF KINDNESS**

QUESTIONS TO ASK YOURSELF:

How can I be kinder to myself each day?

What acts of kindness can I do for others?

What kind things have others done for me?

ACTION:
Spend a day thinking about ways to be kind to yourself and others.

RANDOM ACTS OF KINDNESS

How many tasks can you complete? (There are more tasks on the next page!)

☐ Spend time with a relative	☐ Do some recylcing	☐ Give someone a hug	☐ Smile at somebody
☐ Cook dinner for someone	☐ Make someone a hot drink	☐ Compliment an outfit	☐ Pick up some litter
☐ Hold the door open for someone	☐ Give somebody a compliment	☐ Wish someone good morning	☐ Say Thank you
☐ Help someone with their shopping	☐ Help with housework	☐ Hold someones hand	☐ Dance with somebody

RANDOM ACTS OF KINDNESS

- [ ] Send a nice text
- [ ] Call an old friend or relative
- [ ] Give somebody some flowers
- [ ] Be kind to someone
- [ ] Ask how someones day went
- [ ] Give someone a hug
- [ ] Give someone a gift
- [ ] Listen to someone's problems
- [ ] Make someone laugh
- [ ] Donate to charity
- [ ] Volunteer for something
- [ ] Make someone feel special
- [ ] Leave a kind note
- [ ] Tell someone you appreciate them
- [ ] Water some plants
- [ ] Stroke a pet

CHAMBER OF DREAMS

"If you can dream it, you can do it." - Walt Disney

CHAMBER OF DREAMS

Close your eyes, breathe in slowly, release your shoulders and relax. Walk through the corridors of your mind until you come to the Chamber of Dreams. Find the correct key, turn the lock, open the door and step inside.

Step into the Chamber of Dreams. This is a place for you to explore, express and experience your innermost wishes and dreams. It is a safe space inside your mind where you can think about what you would like in your life. When you are very clear about what you want, you are able to bring it closer and you will have a better opportunity to turn your dreams into reality.

Stand in the centre and notice you are in a circular glass chamber. Projected on the glass are all your wildest dreams and wishes. This is your dream screen. You can add and take away images as your goals and dreams change. On a small table is a remote control. You can use this to add new images. Hold the remote and you see small images flash on its screen. Right swipe any images you want to see on your dream board and left swipe any images you don't wish to have on your dream screen.

Take in a deep breath and breathe out slowly. Close your eyes as you take in another deep breath. On the next out-breath, open your eyes and look at the remote. You see images and symbols flash up on the remote. Right swipe anything you wish to put on your dream board and left swipe anything you don't want on your dream board, remembering that you can bring them back should you change your mind at a later date.

Images of places and countries flash on the remote control and you right or left swipe each one as they appear, deciding what you would like on your dream screen. Continue to breathe in and out slowly as you add images to your dream screen. Buildings flash on the remote and you choose which ones to add. Objects flash on the remote and one by one, you add or take them away from your dream screen. People flash up on the remote and you choose which ones to add. Images of nature flash on the remote and you choose which ones you would like on your dream screen. Images of foods flash on the remote and you make choices as to which you would like on your dream screen. Symbols flash up and you decide what they mean and which ones you would like to right swipe and see on your dream screen. Words flash on the remote and you choose which ones you would like on your dream screen. Feelings such as love, peace, happiness, joy, fear, hurt and anxiety flash on the remote. Choose which ones you want to keep and which you don't want on your dream screen. Colours flash on the remote. Which colours would you like to keep on your dream screen? Thoughts flash on the remote and you make a decision as to which ones you want on your dream screen. Spend some time allowing for any more random images to flash up on your remote.

When the remote control has stopped flashing and the images to choose from have stopped appearing, place it back down and stand in the middle of the chamber. Take time to study closely at the words and images on your dream screen. Look at the words, the symbols and pictures. What feelings do you have when you view your dream screen? How does it make you feel? Take in a deep breath all the way to your stomach and hold on to this feeling as you breathe deeply. Breathe out and let your whole body relax.

You notice there is a notebook and pen on the table. Pick them up and write three goals or small steps you could do to bring your dream closer and bring the feeling to your present life. When you have written your goals, put the notebook and pen down, take one last look at your dream screen, knowing that it will remain here in your dream chamber until you return to add more images and words to it.

"I can create my own destiny; I can create my own destiny."

Write or draw how you feel in your **CHAMBER OF DREAMS**

QUESTIONS TO ASK YOURSELF:

If I had all the money and time in the world, what would I like to do?

What do I want?

What would I love to do in five years time?

ACTION:

Keep a notebook by your bed and note down snippets from your dreams as soon as you wake up. You might start to find themes and messages that will help you.

DREAM BOARD

Cut out pictures from magazines
to create your own dream board.

ChargeUp!

Are you PASSIONATE about helping support young people's emotional wellbeing?

Would you love to help teenagers to be more resilient and confident?

The ChargeUp programme comprises of lessons that focus on helping teens understand and manage their emotional and mental health and wellbeing. covers a wide range of topics from self-awareness, sleep hygiene, to consent and boundaries and stress management.

Sessions follow a 7 step system that includes interesting activities, exercises and games to encourage learning, skill acquisition and reinforcement of concepts. Activities provoke teenagers to think about a range of life skills; from self-awareness, sleep, hygiene, to consent and boundaries and stress management.

Take the ChargeUp Training - For those who want to make a **DIFFERENCE** to the lives of young people

ChargeUp can help develop self-esteem, resilience and assertiveness whilst giving plenty of opportunity for discussion and participation.

Sessions may help young people:

- Improve sleep
- Recharge their system
- Boost confidence
- Improve emotional intelligence
- Give skills to help support themselves and others

AS PART OF THE CHARGEUP TRAINING PROGRAMME YOU WILL RECEIVE:

- Training manual & session plans
- Store credit
- Online resource library - everything you need to run your classes
- Access to online forum

Find out more: www.relaxkids.com/training-info-pack.aspx
training@relaxkids.com

Find us on Facebook: www.facebook.com/groups/RKtraining

www.letsgetcharged.com

IMAGINARIUM DISCUSSION CARDS

Instructions: In groups, pairs or individually - cut out the cards above and put them in either a jar, envelope or bag. Take it in turns to pick a card and then discuss/reflect how you feel when visiting that Chamber.

CONFIDENCE COLLAGE

Use this space to create a picture of confidence. Collect pictures and words from magazines that inspire confidence. Keep your collage and look at it often to remind you to feel and act more confidently.

CHARGEUP RECOMMENDS:

Relax Kids Chill Skills Audio Range

A selection of CDs & MP3s suitable for teens to help build self-esteem, improve confidence, encourage creativity and to help relax and unwind. Purchase online at **www.relaxkids.com**

PowerUp - *Marneta Viegas*

Mental HiiT exercises to help anxiety and stress-management.

This book is full of quick and simple mental exercises designed to bring a few moments of calm and clarity.
Purchase online at **www.relaxkids.com**

FREE AFFIRMATION CALENDAR

Start the day the positive way with our monthly FREE printable affirmation calendar.

Download yours today at
www.relaxkids.com/CU-CALENDAR

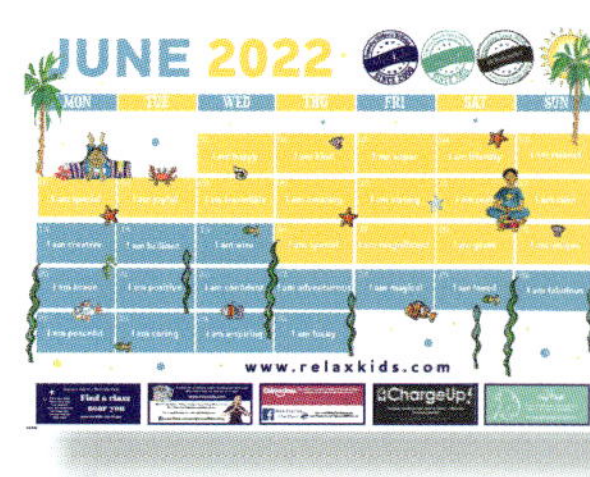

PLEASE NOTE: All products advertised are subject to availability. For further information about our products please visit www.relaxkids.com

Empowering Young Minds

ChargeUp!

www.letsgetcharged.com

www.letsgetcharged.com
www.relaxkids.com